What other professionals say
writin

Natasha's books are thorough and complete for the psychic student. Her down-to-earth and amusing style make spiritual learning accessible and the information easily relatable. I highly recommend both books!

—Rochelle Sparrow, Featured Psychic Trance Channel for ShirleyMacLaine.com

Loved it! Her first book and radio show was a catalyst for me to pursue my own psychic development. Now I'm suddenly psychic! For anyone committed to their spiritual journey, *Aaagh! I Think I'm Psychic* and *Aaagh! I Thought You Were Dead* are a (mostly) fun and a "must" read! Thank you, Natasha!

—Stephan Jacob, Channel Director at Voice America LIVE Internet Talk Radio (stephan.jacob@modavox.com)

In *Aaagh! I Think I'm Psychic,* her stories brought me to tears while inspiring me to continue my own spiritual path, which for a spirit medium can be very challenging. In *Aaagh! I Thought You Were Dead,* Natasha provides above and beyond enlightenment for those who are searching. Natasha's stories are so interesting, I am always disappointed when the book comes to an end. Natasha, you are an inspiration!

—June Field, International Spirit Medium

What Natasha's clients say about her work . . .

I just finished reading your book. It was an incredible adventure. Each chapter guided me to leave behind certain fears and guilts. Your book and wisdom were a gate for forgiveness and liberation of past demons.

—Mila Grandes, Quito, Ecuador

You showed me that the life of my dreams is possible and reminded me that it starts with embracing my wonderful gifts. Everything else will evolve from there.

—Helena, Whistler, Canada

Natasha, you are such a gift to the planet.

—Fran, Hawaii, USA

Wouldn't it be a wonderful world if people would learn and practice the proactive approach to life that Natasha recommends in her column? The world would indeed be a better place.

—Reader, *The Local,* Sunshine Coast, Canada

Thank you for sharing your insights. You always provide hope and you encourage us to have faith in these difficult times.

—Anne, Sunshine Coast, Canada

Natasha told me that my late father was in the room and was saying the word "cancer" which was a gentle warning for my 18-year-old son who immediately understood as he had discovered a tiny lump. He was then scheduled for surgery and was consequently spared the pain of chemotherapy, radiation, and drugs. After being put on a 5-year "surveillance" plan, he is now cancer free. My family and I are in awe of and eternally grateful to Natasha. She is an amazing and talented psychic and medium and her positive energy is inspiring. Clearly, when there are messages that we may not want to hear, she delivers in a gentle way without instilling fear. I now know that our loved ones who have crossed over are our angels who watch over us and will find a way to help if it is a matter of life and death. It takes a very special person to be an assistant to the angels, and Natasha clearly is the best!

—Joanne Lambertsen, Vancouver, Canada

Heartfelt gratitude of the soul-ular kind.

—Anna, Sunshine Coast, Canada

AAAGH!

I THOUGHT YOU WERE DEAD

(And Other Psychic Adventures)

Natasha J. Rosewood

First Edition

Queries regarding rights and permission should be addressed to:

Natasha J. Rosewood
Box 1426
Gibsons, B.C. V0N 1V0

Website: www.natashapsychic.com

Printed by:	Friesens, Winnipeg
Cover Art & Design:	Heather Waddell
Picture:	"Metaman" (www.waddellart.com)
Cover Design & Graphic Art:	Thomas Ziorjen (www.ziorjen.com)
Typesetting:	Fiona Raven
Substantive Editing:	Betty Keller
Copy-Editing/Proofreading:	Judith Hammill
Book Concept & Design:	Natasha J. Rosewood
Photograph:	Raymond Lum (www.raylum.ca)
Creative Director & Make-up Artist:	Angell B. Andersen

Note for Librarians: A cataloguing record for this book that includes Dewey Classification and US Library of Congress numbers is available from the National Library of Canada. The complete cataloguing record can be obtained from the National Library's online database at: www.nlc-bnc.ca/amicus/index-e.html

ISBN 978-0-973-4711-1-3

Printed in Canada

Other Titles by Natasha J. Rosewood . . .

AAAGH! I THINK I'M PSYCHIC
(And You Can Be Too)

COMING SOON:

INTO THE VALLEY OF DEATH
(And Other Ghost Stories)

ABOVE THE CLOUDS

Come into My Parlor

"Come into my parlor," said the spider to the fly.
"Just because you can't see all with your earthly eye
doesn't mean spirits don't exist or that you'll ever die.
You might think that you're merely a speck of dust,
that life is meaningless, of little worth, but you can trust
that you have more impact and you are greater than you think.
You're on the edge of a new world. Yes, right on the brink
where every living cell's fate is determined by what it thinks.
So forgive your past, open your heart, and to all be kind.
Let this new heaven on earth blossom through the power of your mind."

—Natasha J. Rosewood

What Is This Book About?

"Do you see dead people?" a new client once asked Natasha.
"Oh, yes. All the time," she responded. "And so can you . . . if you are open."

But seeing spirits is only a small element of Natasha Rosewood's life as a psychic development coach, spiritual healer, and writer. In this fast-paced book about Natasha's psychic adventures, she takes the reader on a roller-coaster ride of fascinating and poignant, gut-wrenching and joyful, thought-provoking and hope-filled experiences. As in her first book, *Aaagh! I Think I'm Psychic (And You Can Be Too),* her intention in writing is to strengthen our trust in our inherent intuitiveness. In these twenty based-on-true tales of this psychic's personal and professional life, the sometimes funny, sometimes dramatic, and other times miraculous stories explore metaphysics from all dimensions. Mysteries such as how we can live in quantum consciousness, what happens after we die, where animal spirits go, what soul retrieval is, how cellular memory affects us, and other unknowns are explored and resolved.

The *Dear Natasha* questions that follow each story are the inquiries most often posed by Natasha's international and eclectic clientele. Her concise responses to those questions, based on her thirty years as a metaphysician, offer an interpretation of how quantum physics can interact with our psychology, our ever-evolving spirituality, our higher power, and the illusory, spirit-based world in which we all live.

Not only do Natasha's experiences deepen our understanding of how the spirit world interfaces with our physical world but her stories show us how we can commune with our deceased loved ones. When fear of the invisible is no longer a barrier and we are willing to embrace the concept of a never-ending existence, we can forgive more easily, express our love more generously, and heal unresolved issues from current or past lifetimes more quickly. Readers will be encouraged to open their minds and their hearts to eternity and hope. By developing their own sensitivities to spirit, metaphysical explorers will not only have a broader appreciation of how the psychic realm works but they will also be able to see, feel, and heal their own spirits.

Join Natasha Rosewood in *Aaagh! I Thought You Were Dead (And Other Psychic Adventures)* for the journey of many lifetimes.

How to Get the Most Out of This Book . . .

My Intention. The purpose of this book is to open readers' minds to the eternity of life and the magic of their own minds so they may understand how to use universal energies for their highest good. In the process, I hope as always to empower and entertain as well as enlighten. The chapters, therefore, have been broken down into two parts: the stories and the *Dear Natasha* questions and answers that follow each story. These are the most common queries posed by my clients. My responses to the questions are intended as a metaphysical, spiritual, psychological, quantum-consciousness teaching to elaborate on the preceding story.

Some readers of my first book, *Aaagh! I Think I'm Psychic*—in which I used a similar format—preferred to first absorb the stories while skipping over the teachings. Once they had read the main chapters straight through, they then returned to absorb the stories *and* the teachings. Try it your way, whatever that may be, and see!

Your Beliefs. I have not written either of these books to beat you, dear reader, over the head with my beliefs nor to discredit any religion or credo about our spiritual journey. These stories are based on my own personal and professional experiences as a psychic. I will, of course, only see my experiences through my own set of perceptions. Our beliefs, whatever they may be, serve us in some way until they are no longer valid, and then we change them. If this book offends you, therefore, know that it was not the author's intention. (Just leave the book at the local funeral home.) I will not apologize for expressing my truth. If it is also your truth, you will recognize it. Validation, peace, freedom, relief, and even joy may resonate within you. What I do hope is that these writings will empower you to forgive and heal your old hurts and/or aid you in communing with loved ones, alive or dead. Some of the stories might put a smile on your face or even make you cry. Mostly I hope that my writing will inspire you to live freely in the moment, without guilt, and to know that no one is dead, because life is eternal. It is never "too late" to love and be loved.

Awomen/Amen!

Acknowledgments

Divine Thanks and Gratitude go to:

- The spirits of the adults, children, and other beings who inspired the stories in this book. I commend all these people for their bravery, extra-ordinariness, open-mindedness, and grace as they continue with their exceptional lives. Thank you for being examples of courage, faith, and hope.
- My family and friends for being there through the great and the not-so-great times. You know who you are.
- All my clients, who along with friends and family, have honored me by opening up their souls and allowing me to see their essences. I am truly blessed with a family of clients who are a continuing source of learning, teaching, inspiration, and confirmation of my gifts. Thank you all for your patience while waiting for this second book. If you promise to slow down your reading pace, I will increase the speed of my writing!
- All the talented people who have contributed to the final production of this book:
- Betty Keller, Writing Guru Extraordinaire and Substantive Editor
- Judith Hammill, Ms. Picky-Picky Copy-Editor, Support, and Friend
- Fiona Raven, oh-so-patient Book Layout and Design Implementer
- Heather Waddell, Cover Artist whose beautiful and intriguing art works continue to draw people to my writing
- Thomas Ziorjen, efficient Cover Designer and Graphic Artist
- Raymond Lum, kind Photographer
- Angell Andersen, miracle worker Make-up Artist
- George (Jorge) Rocha, Friesens, for excellent Sales and Support
- All the readers of my first book, especially those who sent me wonderful testimonials and thereby inspire me to keep writing
- My own spirit guides, angels, deceased friends, and other divinities who not only channel wisdom and healing through me but also let me take the credit for much of their guidance
- All the baristas who have allowed me to write for hours in their establishments while nursing just one cup of coffee, especially Wheatberries, Gibsons, Canada, and The Coffee Co., Carmel, California.

Disclaimer

While these stories are inspired by actual events, most of the names, characters, places, incidents, and some establishments have been changed to honor the privacy of each EXCEPT where the person or establishment has given express permission to use real names (marked by * asterisks). Some stories are an amalgamation of my clients' experiences and have been included because of their universal truths and their teaching values. While many readers may think they recognize themselves within these pages, the names, places, and dialogue are either the product of the author's imagination or if real are used fictitiously. Any resemblance to events, locales, or actual persons living or dead is entirely coincidental.

While friends, family, and some of my clients are the inspirations for these stories, and are aware of this, the writings are my perceptions of the events as I experienced them from my professional psychic's point of view. As such, they are merely meant to serve as examples of how every one of us can evolve spiritually by understanding how metaphysics positively impacts us. The characters in my book are the other cast members in my "movie" and are, therefore, my teachers. I have tried to honor them as such.

On occasion you will notice that I have, in the *Dear Natasha* sections, randomly chosen to use "he" or "she" rather than use "he/she." My choice of gender does not reflect any bias toward or against either gender in any way but has been used merely as a means to make the reading more fluent.

Out of the Mouths of Babes

A conversation between two psychics—one professional and one nine-year-old Indigo child:

Celestina: Auntie, what do you think life is all about?

Aunt: Well, Celie, I think it's like a school. We all come here to learn our lessons about love. If we don't learn them, we have to keep coming back until we get them right. Then we can move on to higher dimensions. What do you think life is all about?

Celestina: I think life is like an offer.

Aunt: What do you mean?

Celestina: I think offers come to us out of the ether. We have the choice to accept them or refuse them. If we refuse them, they go away again, back into the ether.

Contents

Foreword

Rochelle Sparrow, MSW
Psychic Trance Channel

Accepting our abilities to communicate with spirit requires us to step into ourselves and honor what we find present. It is a journey not for the faint of heart, but for the heroines and heroes who courageously move forward to embrace the reality of their existence. It requires us to become honest witnesses to how we truly experience the world in which we live. Our honesty may leave us feeling vulnerable, alone, and possibly different from those around us.

It is our perceived differences that Natasha skillfully and humorously addresses. In *Aaagh! I Thought You Were Dead*, Natasha points out the processes we all move through in accepting our psychic ability. She normalizes common fears and helps reassure us that we are not alone in our experience. She helps us to understand the impact upon our current reality of flexible energy, of past lives, and of those who have passed on. She acts as a wise guide to lead us to see more of who we are and what we can become. Natasha shows us a picture of spirit we may not have seen before.

So if you are ready to open your connection with spirit through understanding more of how spirit speaks to us, if you are willing to delve into yourself to know more about who you are and to develop your connection with spirit, this book has been written with you in mind.

I invite you on a journey, a journey that is exciting, maybe a little startling, perhaps not what you thought it was going to be. But any journey worth taking is never what you thought it was going to be at the beginning, is it? *Aaagh! I Thought You Were Dead* will lead you down the path to something more. I highly recommend you step forward.

—Rochelle Sparrow, Psychic Trance Channel, MSW, Author, Media Personality, Event Speaker. Featured channel for shirleymaclaine.com
rochellesparrow@yahoo.com
Now on www.myspace.com/rochellesparrow
www.myspace.com/sparrowkaneventures
Phone: 602.430.6447

FAMOUS AND INFAMOUS GHOSTS

"You have to come!" My old friend Georgia was demanding my presence in Halifax. "It'll be a west coast wussie reunion, and we have to see Sandy's mythical new 'dar-r-r-rn' ocean-side cottage in Pugwash, or wherever the hell it is." Georgia always mimicked everyone, but was really funny when she copied Sandy's Nova Scotian brogue.

Georgia, Sandy, and I had met in Whistler in the early '90s, but Georgia had moved to New York and Sandy had moved back to her native Nova Scotia. Due to the ten years' difference in our ages, I had named us the Bronze (Georgia), Silver (me), and Golden (Sandy) Girls, and Sandy had called Georgia and me west coast wussies because we were afraid of the frigid June Pacific Ocean waters. But despite our total irreverence for each other, when we were together we laughed incessantly.

A week in Halifax, Nova Scotia, in July could be fun, I thought. I would get to see the old city that I had heard so much about from Sandy. And it would provide an opportunity to launch my first and self-published book, *Aaagh! I Think I'm Psychic (And You Can Be Too)*, on the east coast. If I could persuade a couple of Halifax bookstores to sell it, then I could honestly claim that my book was available from coast to coast. Flying from the west to the east coast, a journey that would take longer than traveling from one continent to another, would then be worth the cost. One day in Halifax would give me enough time to visit the bookstores I had already researched, and then Sandy would come and "git" me in the early evening and take me to join the others. So that was the plan.

"Oh, you *must* stay at the *Waverley Inn, dah-ling," my friend Carmela responded in her very British accent when I asked her which hotel I should choose for my one-night stay in Halifax. Apart from having good taste, she was also an expert on Nova Scotia. As she punched in the website on her laptop, she added, "It's just luh-verly. Look."

Even as the pictures of the Waverley Inn popped up on her computer screen and I was able to voyeuristically preview the property over Carmela's shoulder, I could see the place was oh so haunted. Those pixels that made up the colored pictures of the rooms danced on the computer screen as if they were full of live, conscious particles. But that otherworldly energy, I decided, did not feel dark or even like heavy-duty ghosts. They had merely taken up residence. I could live with them, for one night anyway.

And soon I was standing in front of the elegant entrance of the Waverley Inn while the driver unloaded my suitcase. It was nine at night, local time, which for this west coaster meant five in the evening. A four-hour time change and 14 hours of air, sea, and land travel from Vancouver was not enough to send an ex-flight attendant like me straight to bed. Perhaps I would explore.

Even at the reception desk in the large open hallway, I could feel the air thick with the spirits of former guests now invisible to the human eye. Then as I rolled my suitcase down the red-carpeted corridor, lined with its cream-painted doorways and a bumpy old floor beneath, I noticed a wide staircase going up to the left. The large gilt-framed oil paintings hanging on the wall were presumably of deceased relatives or noted Halifax characters. Although the bright red carpet exuded warmth, just a slightly darker red tinge would have easily made the atmosphere more ominous. The hotel's decorators, I decided, had quite artfully walked a fine line between a home for retired vampires and an old-world-charming bed and breakfast.

As soon as I entered my room, the last one at the end of the corridor, all the spirits crowded in on me. They, like many dead people, love getting an audience with a psychic. And who can blame them? Living people always need to be seen and heard. And a lot of dead people too are busting to communicate with their still-living loved ones. Psychics are the lucky conduits.

Although most of us *can* commune with the dead without the services of a medium, in our western culture we are notoriously bad at listening even to the living, so what chance do the dead have of being heard? As the spirits surged toward me, I had the feeling I often have at the end of my bookstore talks when everyone approaches at once with their questions and a hunger in their eyes for answers. If I had allowed the entities in that room to talk to me all at once, *and* if I had listened, a straight jacket might have been in order. But I didn't. "Guys, leave me alone," I instructed them telepathically but then added out loud for more emphasis, "I'm tired and I'm going to have a bath. Go away." Just because psychics are good listeners doesn't mean we don't also need a rest sometimes.

I sensed a collective metaphysical groan of disappointment. But I didn't care.

After soaking in the very narrow bathtub in the very narrow bathroom, which I suspect was squished in as an ensuite-afterthought, I lay on the downy bed and sampled the luxury of wrap-around-the-neck down pillows. Ah, heaven! I was tempted to lie there and watch mind-numbing programs on television but something in that room was making me restless. *If I relax*, I thought, *the spirits might still try to commune after all.* Though none of them was aggressive, downright miserable, or clanking chains, I could feel their presence, waiting, hoping I would eventually relent. I decided I would get no peace, so I got dressed and went in search of a bowl of hot soup.

"There's a pub just down the street," the receptionist responded when I asked about food. "*The Henry House."

I thanked her and picked my way in the dark along badly lit, uneven pavement. The Henry House was an old three-storey brick building and as I ascended the few steps to the front door, I saw the lights of the pub below street level. As a female traveling solo, I wasn't relishing the idea of eating alone, especially in a pub. But, oh well, it was all part of the adventure.

Walking into the Henry House was just like walking into someone's home. The long, high-ceilinged hallway with its wooden floor and carpeted staircase rising to the right was reminiscent of English and Scottish houses. Straight ahead was the bar with a young male bartender polishing glasses, preparing to close for the night.

"The pub's downstairs," he said, pointing to a single wooden door under the broad staircase.

I hesitated. "Would it be okay if I just stayed up here? I just want a glass of white wine and a bowl of soup. I'm not really that comfortable in pubs by myself," I admitted.

"Sure." He shrugged and pointed to the far end of the bar. "Grab a seat."

As I climbed up on a stool, my back was to the empty restaurant, and the door to the pub was under the staircase in front of me.

"Sauvignon blanc okay?" the bartender asked.

"Yes, thank you."

Apart from the bartender and a mature woman with short curly hair and glasses who was working with him, I was the only person at the bar. The restaurant behind me was somberly lit, full of round wooden tables all set up for the next day's customers. As I glanced over to the wide staircase with its wooden banister, I wondered how old the building was and who had lived here before.

The woman came over and handed me a large white laminated menu.

"Actually, I just want a bowl of soup," I said.

"French onion or clam chowder?" she offered.

Even though I knew the clam chowder would probably be really good in this part of the world, I ordered my favorite, French onion. As I waited, happy just to sit and absorb my surroundings, I eavesdropped on the people behind the bar as they talked about needed supplies, the customers of the day, and local gossip. Their soft voices were relaxing, and maybe the white wine was starting to take the edge off my travel fatigue.

Suddenly in the hallway ahead of me, I heard a swishing noise. When I peered at the space where the noise came from, I saw a flash of a young woman wearing a velvet cape over a crinoline dress. The hood of the cape was pulled up over her head obscuring her face as she paced up and down the hallway. She was about nineteen years old and very upset. Her agitation, I felt, was caused by her father. He didn't approve of her, had no respect or love for her, and she was greatly disturbed by his rejection. Her despair at not having her father's love was causing her restlessness, her pain. The ghost of this poor young woman, I felt, had been pacing for well over 100 years. Her father was apparently a very important man. Then I saw him.

He was standing halfway up the staircase, a big, imposing man. Other important people, mainly men, were standing around and below him on the stairs. He was speaking, holding court, his audience spellbound by his words. The house I sensed belonged to one of the other men, who hosted many parties here. Then I understood from the energy of the first man that, although he cared well for his daughter's physical needs, he largely ignored her because he perceived her to be lacking in intelligence, possibly because she was female.

The woman who had taken my order and who was now taking stock behind the bar was, I presumed, the manager if not the owner of the premises. As she handed me my soup, I asked her, "Is this place haunted?"

Although she flinched, she concentrated hard on the hot bowl and managed to put it safely down in front of me. "Why do you ask?"

"I sense ghosts here. I'm psychic."

"People tell me it is," she said, then hesitated. "Would I be disturbing you if we talked?"

"Not at all," I responded.

She came around the bar and offered her hand as she climbed onto the stool beside me. "My name is *Donna. I'm the owner."

"Natasha Rosewood."

"Are you just visiting Halifax?"

"Yes. I'm here to put my book in bookstores."

"Oh . . . what's the name of your book?"

"*Aaagh! I Think I'm Psychic (And You Can Be Too).*"

She smiled. "Hmmm. It's funny you should say the house is haunted. A television crew is coming here soon to make a documentary on local ghosts. They're filming in a few places in Halifax. Henry House is just one of them." Glancing around, she added, almost to herself, "I hope they don't short-circuit the place with all their huge lights." She turned back to face me. "A haunted house on the other side of Halifax burned down while they were shooting." She frowned. "I know the wiring in this place can't handle it."

"Maybe the electricity wasn't the reason it burned down," I suggested. "Stranger things have happened when ghosts have been intruded upon." She gave me a sidelong glance. "Just ask them to use an auxiliary power unit for their lighting," I added to reassure her. After a small taste of the hot soup, I asked, "Do you live here, too?"

"Yes, my husband and I live on the third floor," she said, raising her eyes upward toward the staircase. "It's a very old house and has quite the history. But tell me, what do you see?"

Between mouthfuls of piping hot, deliciously cheesy soup, I described the young woman pacing up and down the hallway. "Do you ever feel her?" I asked Donna.

"Sometimes when I'm down here alone at night doing the books, I can feel a presence, but I haven't seen anyone," she admitted. "Not so far." Even in the shadowy light of the bar, I could see that Donna was now alert to my visions, but she wasn't yet ready to reveal her story. It was okay—I was used to being tested. "Anything else?" she probed.

Then I described the girl's father, the man on the staircase.

"That's amazing! Martin," she said, addressing the male bartender, "this woman *really* is psychic." Then she tapped me on the arm. "Come here a minute."

She led me over to the hallway and on the wall below the staircase she pointed to a faded, sepia-toned photo showing two rows of men, the back row standing, the front sitting. "Is that him?" Donna asked, pointing to the figure standing in the center.

"I think so . . . ." I frowned and peered more closely at the photograph. "No, *that's* him," I said pointing to the tall figure standing next to the man in the center. "But—Ohmigod! Aren't those men—?"

She smiled. "Yes, the Fathers of Confederation. The man in the center is William Alexander Henry, one of the two men who penned the British North America Act. He owned this house, you know," she added proudly. "It was while he was here that he wrote the Articles of Confederation."

"And that's John A. MacDonald, isn't it?" I asked, pointing to the well-known face.

"Yes, Sir John A. MacDonald," Donna corrected me. I continued staring at his lean face.

"He was definitely the man I saw on the stairs!"

Donna nodded, smiling. "We don't have any documentation he was here, but it's possible, even probable. The Fathers of Confederation held three historical meetings—in London, Quebec City, and Charlottetown. It would have made sense for them to stay here and leave from Halifax for London and even for Prince Edward Island."

We returned to our seats where I finished my soup while Donna filled me in on other details. Apparently, William Henry had had a reputation for hosting parties in this house and enjoying his tipple. Holding court on the staircase with the major players was a scene likely to have taken place in those days of Confederation-planning.

"Do you get anything else about the house?" Donna persisted as I scraped crusty cheesy remnants from the bowl.

"I'm sure there are tons of ghosts here." Jet lag was beginning to take its toll and I wasn't getting specifics. "In fact, this whole street is haunted. I'm staying at the Waverley Inn up the road, and the atmosphere is thick with spirit energy."

"Yes," she replied as she signed off on a requisition for the bartender, "the town of Halifax is well-known for its ghosts. But what about here?"

"Let me see," I tuned in again. "Oh—"

"What?" Donna leaned forward.

"In this room,"—I waved my arm toward the restaurant behind me. The tables were configured in almost the same pattern, but I was seeing a different era.—"there are a lot of men . . . from the higher echelons of Halifax society . . . dressed in tuxes . . . at the tables playing cards and drinking . . . but the women are all in black with red bustiers, and their hair is piled on top . . . . Oh, it's a brothel!"

The bartender was now leaning on the bar listening, fascinated by our conversation. Donna looked at him with a conspiratorial smile.

"After William Alexander Henry sold the place," she explained almost breathless, "it was turned into a brothel. When we bought the house years later, it was in bad shape."

"How did you come to buy the house?" I asked, always curious about how people find their destinies.

"Actually, that's a story in itself. It found us . . . through a friend. We weren't even thinking of buying a pub, let alone in Halifax. But this man we know contacted us in Toronto after having been here and told us we should get out here and buy the place. Of course, we didn't take him seriously. But then coincidentally another friend invited us to a wedding, which happened to take place at the Waverley Inn right next door. And when we saw this place, something just told us that we had to buy it."

"I do believe all houses have spirits, and it's the spirits of those houses that choose the owners. They just let us think we have the power to choose. But I think we're picked and then we get sucked in."

"Do you think so?"

"And maybe . . . and I know this sounds a little far-fetched . . . ," I smiled only half-joking, "you're the reincarnation of that young woman, the daughter of Sir John A. MacDonald. You've come back to make peace with yourself."

Donna just stared at me, not refuting the idea but not accepting it either. "I'll have to think about that theory," she replied. "But I do know one thing, Natasha . . . ."

"What's that?"

"I need to buy your book."

As I gingerly picked my way amongst the crooked paving stones back to the haunted Waverley Inn, praying that I would enjoy a peaceful night's sleep, I wondered if hotels also pick their guests, the live ones as well as the deceased.

1 Is It Possible to Change the Past?

Dear Natasha,

My home is haunted by a ghost but sometimes I wonder if the ghost is an aspect of me. And if it is, is it possible to change the past and stop being haunted?

Dear Stuck-in-the-Past,

Unforgiven guilt, anger, and hurt can cause spirits—alive or dead—to stay attached to the past until the person is forgiven, validated, and released. Guilt can be a useful emotion but only if we use it to propel our consciences forward into affirmative action. Sadly, most of us use guilt to keep us glued to an unhappy past—or use it to become unglued in the present. Guilt then *becomes* the ghost.

According to The Foundation of Inner Peace in their book *A Course in Miracles,* when we believe in our guilt we also believe we deserve punishment, and then fear of that punishment plagues us. Living in a vibration of constant fear attracts even more negativity into our lives which, because of our guilt, we believe we deserve. Living in a stuck past, therefore, paralyzes us into a destructive, repetitive loop until the guilt is released and we can step fully into an innocent present. When we forgive ourselves (and other characters in our movie, no matter what misdeeds they might have committed against us), we are more likely to change our perception of our past. Having forgiven the guilt, we can then relinquish the perceived need for punishment. In that mindset, we are then free to live in a present that has unlimited potential.

So yes, you can change the past, if you are ready and willing.

Ghosts or guilt haunt us in many different ways. Feelings of guilt can fester inside us and can also make us prone to attracting troubled ghosts of similar vibration. One of the following ghost-types may explain your haunting:

* **Imprints** are often mistaken for ghosts but their essence is not really there. They are merely a residual echo of our spirit energy and have only a faint emotional attachment to the place, person, or object connected to the event. Still, the stronger the emotion is *at the time of the occurrence*, the stronger the imprint. (See Chapter 3: "Psychic Break-In.")

* **Witness spirits** hang around the living whether or not they have any relationship to them—but are not ghosts. In order to progress through the spirit world or to prepare for their next incarnation, the witness

spirit is often reviewing a lesson left unfulfilled while they lived. They are merely learning vicariously from a living being who has a similar lesson to learn.

* **Ghosts** are much heavier, stuck energies with unresolved emotional issues. They tend to remain attached to the person, property, object, and land that is familiar to them, or where the (mis)deed occurred. Whether ghosts occupy our homes or are stranded pieces of our own souls, these miserable essences often try to get our attention through physical activity in the hope that we will help them become unstuck. Ghosts also like to congregate with other ghosts so they can be seen by each other—and because misery loves company!

As like attracts like, **ghosts** can also be drawn to someone living with the same unhappy issues. This might be the type of haunting you are referring to and is illustrated in the preceding story.

But why do ghosts exist?

The Universe does not force ghosts or live spirits to "just get over" their emotional obstacles. We have been given free will so we can *choose when* to face the issue and move on . . . or not. The soul is eternal so there is no rush to heal. But who wants to suffer for eternity? Ghosts will haunt, replaying the event over and over again until they are tired of being stuck in the same old loop. As with the living, only when these lost souls are ready to forgive and accept forgiveness will they allow themselves to move forward and step into a higher and lighter experience.

Whether your ghost is within or without or both, you *can* relinquish your guilt and your ghost. While I always recommend seeking professional guidance, here are some steps that you can take:

1. Focus on compassion, first for yourself and then for the perpetrators of past deeds.
2. Bring your guilt to consciousness, whether your guilt is valid or not. For example, perhaps you were just an innocent child when a sibling died and you absorbed the guilt.
3. Forgive yourself. Many decisions are made out of a survival instinct, a shock reaction to the circumstances, or a lack of accurate information at the time.
4. Release the pain of what others did to you by refusing to give them your power any longer. If *you* are still carrying the pain of *their* deeds, you are still giving your power to their actions. Stop it!

5. Honor your process and accept your actions—instead of continuing to berate yourself for the past. Let go of the *If-only-I-had* . . . .
6. Develop a constructive meaning for what took place and create a new perception of your past. In some weird way, the event is a gift of learning.
7. Don't take the event as a personal affront. Decide that what happened was just a loving Universe trying to get your attention and wake you up to a more powerful you. Although it is a personal experience, the Universe isn't out to get you.
8. Explore the concept that your waking state is merely an illusion of your own making. Only your dreams tell the truth. Choose your own illusion.
9. Empower yourself. Make good, if not to the injured person, then to yourself and/or to someone who *can* benefit. Pay it forward.
10. Recognize that you are powerful and that your power lies in choosing to embrace and learn from your past.
11. Call on your angels to help your inner ghost or guilt find resolution and be at peace. Once *you* are healed, your outer ghost will leave, either to go "home" in peace or to seek alternative miserable company.
12. Decide that before you let go of your past, you will first replace your pain with joy. If what we focus on expands—and you are focused on joy—there will be no room for pain or guilt.

So, **dear Stuck-in-the-Past**, to be at peace, all we have to do is keep moving forward in grace and with compassion, knowing that the present is all there is and we are all one. At any given moment, we are choosing what we perceive as our reality. Rather than wading in the heavy mud of destructive thinking, why not focus on a lighter, more magical experience. Decide to be at peace. Everything is in divine right order. You are safe and all is well in your world. No more ghosts!

THE DEAD PEOPLE PARTY

"It'll be fun," my friend Sarah said. "We'll make it a Hallowe'en party. Can you manage seven people?"

Yes, live ones, I thought, having an eerie, clairvoyant moment. We were talking about a psychic party in Victoria where I would go to her home and offer thirty-minute psychic readings to her friends.

On a Wednesday evening two weeks later, Sarah showed me into her large pink bedroom. While her five- and eight-year-old daughters watched wide-eyed from their parents' king-sized bed, I organized two chairs and set up my psychic kit—tissues, crystals, candles, tape deck, tapes, business cards, angel cards, and fairy cards—on a small table. Once the mother had taken her two girls into their own rooms, I invited my first "victim" into my parlor.

Primarily, the readings were uneventful—for a psychic, anyway. The fourth lady to come into the room was Jody, and I warmed immediately to the sparkle in her dark eyes. As always before I begin a reading, I outlined my philosophy and explained briefly where the information comes from, reminding her to take all my predictions with a grain of salt.

N: *You were married?*
J: *Yes.*
N: *He's still around you . . . a lot.*
J: (smiling) *He probably is.*
N: *He's passed on then?*

Sometimes when a "dead" spirit is active on the physical plane, it is difficult to tell whether they are actually alive or have passed. Conversely, some living people's spirits are so dead it feels as if they are long gone!

J: *Yes.*

N: *Oh, this is interesting. He's telling me that he's getting ready to reincarnate or go onto another level. Before he does, he wants to make sure that you're all taken care of. He wants you to remarry. He says it's time.*

J: *He's right. It's been five years.*

N: (laughing) *He's telling me that he's been looking for someone to replace himself but has been having a heck of a time finding anyone as good as he is.*

J: (chuckling) *That sounds like him.*

N: *But he has found someone now and he's pushing the two of you together.*

J: *Yes, I think I'm ready now.*

Often spirits have difficulty coming down to our level of vibration and the communication can be like a static radio or a television on the blink, but this spirit was clear with a strong presence.

N: *What is your husband's name?*

J: *Daniel.*

N: *This new man doesn't live here. He's in Vancouver. And you will meet him at a party . . . a Christmas party.*

J: *So soon?*

N: *It could be this Christmas, but my timing can be off so it could be later. Your husband is showing me a red cocktail dress and telling me that you should wear it to this party. Has he always taken charge like this?*

J: *In a good way. He wasn't a control freak or anything. But he always told me that if anything happened to him, he would want me to remarry.*

N: *Well, he's really pushing this man at you. He wants you to wear the red dress. Did he give you diamond earrings?*

J: *No, but I have some.*

N: *Wear those. And he says you look really cute with your hair up.*

J: (throws head back and laughs) *He used to say that!*

N: *Something about lots of chest hair. Did he have red hair?*

J: *Yes, Irish as they come.*

N: *This new man is very like Daniel, and I feel it will be an almost instant attraction. But you must remember he isn't your husband and try not to expect him to be.* He *is* him *and he is different. I feel his wife left him or died. And I see an eight-year-old girl around you that I believe he will bring in. She desperately needs a mothering energy, and I see you giving that to her and doing a good job.*

Jody nodded as if accepting the assignment.

N: *You have a son around 16 who loves to play rugby?*
J: *He loves to watch it.*
N: *Your husband is pushing your son out the door and telling him to get his butt in gear. He warns him not to just watch but also play. This new man will be good for your son, particularly as he is really missing his father.*
J: (heaves a huge sigh of relief) *Yes, I've been having a lot of problems with him. Roger, Sarah's husband, has offered to step in.*
N: *That's good. He needs a male mentor. All your children love the new man. He's a natural Dad. Lots of fun. Great sense of humor. I get the name Peter, but please don't just date Peters!*

I then tried to continue doing a palm reading, explaining the lines to Jody, but her husband's presence was so strong that he overwhelmed any other energy. I finally surrendered to him and continued to act as medium. He had both of us, client and psychic, in stitches laughing. Finally I thanked him for coming through so vividly and with such clear information. Although Daniel had entertained us and no doubt offered some healing to Jody, the night was not over.

Diane was my next client. She'd had to put her cat down that morning. Her dulled brown eyes and quivering voice pulled on my heart as she asked me if I could tune in to his departed spirit. Feeling her rawness but helpless to offer more comfort, I apologized and told her that I felt the cat was still "in transition." Newly departed spirits are sometimes just not available to commune with the living as they are also dealing with their own death and rebirth into the spirit world. Her cat, I felt, just wasn't yet ready to come through. "Come back in three months," I told her. I felt bad as she left the room emotionally heavy with disappointment.

Valerie was the seventh and last reading of the night. Maybe it was because I was getting tired but something about her cool Nordic features made me think that she might be harder to read than the others. "The lifeline represents our vitality, our life force, our way of being in the world," I was explaining when, on the Mount of Venus, the name "Doug" appeared.

N: *Do you know someone who has passed on with the name Doug?*
V: (glances to her left, mentally scanning her list of acquaintances) *No.*
N: (shrugging telepathically, I push "Doug" to the side so I can continue with her reading) *Whatever you are doing now for a career, it feels as if there will be a change within the next two years . . . . Are you sure you don't know a Doug? He's come back and he's quite persistent.*
V: (frowning) *I can't think of anyone by that name.*
N: *Okay, well, we'll get back to him later.*

Then as I moved to study the Mount of the Moon in the lower palm, suddenly I heard in my mind "*Doug!*" being yelled at me. I jumped back from my client. Valerie also pulled suddenly back from me, her eyes wide and frightened with an *Is-she-quite-mad?* stare.

N: *It's Doug again. He just won't go away.*

Then in a much calmer voice, I heard the words "not very tall" and was shown a bald head. Finally it dawned on me. *Oh! It's Doug!* I thought. He was *my* contact and communing with *me*. I decided I should explain this carefully to my client so she didn't think I was completely crazy.

N: *This is strange. Doug is a friend's brother. He died last week and he's coming through your palm. And so soon! It's unusual for new spirits to do that unless they're restless. But he's not restless.*

Valerie was still frowning, confused by my ramblings.

N: *Doug is pointing to an older man. Have you lost a grandfather in the last year?*
V: *My grandfather died six months ago.* (She sits forward again.)
N: *Mmmm? He's not settled, not at peace yet.*
V: (nodding) *Yes, there are some problems. And I think I know what it is or who it is that's causing the problems.*
N: *The grandfather believes it's his fault for not making something irrevocably clear in his will, something ambiguous that could be taken both ways and cause misappropriation.*

V: *His wife . . . she's difficult and she could legally go two ways. Yes.*

Doug reappeared holding a door open as if he were a gatekeeper. Through the door, on the other side, I could see a taller, older man, the grandfather, fretting. Doug was holding and stroking a large cat. "The cat's okay," I heard him say. Diane would be happy to hear that. Then as if Doug were facilitating the communication between granddaughter and grandfather, he opened the door even wider and pointed to the grandfather.

N: *Your grandfather won't rest until everyone gets what he wanted them to have, especially you.*
V: (sighs) *Yes. There's a lot of stuff to be sorted.*

I wanted to offer Valerie more words of comfort but the grandfather seemed as helpless and frustrated as she did. And there wasn't time that night to sort it all out. The message was that she would just have to go through the process and, hopefully, eventually the grandfather would find peace.

Several aspects of Doug's spirit's appearance were surprising. How he so forcefully made his presence felt and would not tolerate being ignored was a first for me. Secondly, I had never been yelled at by a spirit before! And thirdly, it is rare for a spirit that has so recently left the physical plane to act as communicator on behalf of the spirit world. In my experience, it takes the new arrivals a little time to readjust before they begin acting as guides.

What struck me was his coolness, as if he had been the gatekeeper forever. He acted as if it were the most natural thing in the world that he, the spirit of my friend's dead brother, should show up in a complete stranger's palm, demand attention, and then calmly act as chaperone for the spirits of a dead cat and an unsettled grandfather.

Doug, as much as I knew of him, wasn't even particularly spiritual in his life and didn't even believe in the psychic realm. But perhaps I didn't know him as well as I thought I did, and he was an old soul who had just come to be my helper. Who was I to refuse or even question it? I'll take all the help I can get.

After Valerie's reading was done and she had left the room, I silently asked Doug if he had any messages for his own family. He responded almost nonchalantly by saying that it was unnecessary to say anything to them. Everything in the family was understood. He knew they all loved him and he loved them. Like an angel, his motives in helping were totally selfless.

What a dead people party!

2 Why Can't I See My Dead Husband?

Dear Natasha,

My husband died suddenly four years ago of a heart attack. Psychics tell me he is around me but how can I see him myself?

Dear Not Seeing,

You are not alone in your quest! And yes, I feel your husband is with you. Often when we want to see something so badly, our fear of *not* seeing gets in the way. The job of the ego-mind—or pea-brain as I like to call it—is to keep our fears alive and well, to keep us in the illusion of being separate and small. The ego will attempt to talk us out of the bigger truth.

We need to trust our inner voices which many of us believe are "just our imagination." When we can *let go of our attachment* to the outcome—which in your case is needing to feel your late husband's love—often the outcome appears. To experience communication with spirit, we need to be willing to trust that life is eternal and that we can see, feel, hear, touch, and know the invisible. Just because we don't see something with the human eye doesn't mean it doesn't exist.

Disembodied spirits are vibrating at a much higher frequency than our body-encased spirits in the denser physical plane in which we live. When we bypass the ego-mind and open up in silence to our higher frequency, we can tune in on the same vibration as spirit and make it easier for them to communicate with us.

So, **dear Not Seeing,** the following is what I use to commune with spirit. It works! If you practice this process, I am sure you will be able to see/feel/hear your husband.

1. Put yourself in a quiet state and take three deep breaths from your solar plexus (stomach), and then relax into even breathing.
2. Remind yourself that you are spirit/mind/consciousness/thought with a physical casing.
3. Think about your lost loved one. Imagine him in your mind.
4. Allow yourself to remember his energy, the feeling of his being with you.
5. Invite him to be with you in a mutually remembered place now.

6. Tell him in your mind silently or out loud what you want to communicate.
7. Then—and this is the really important part—***listen***! Gently push your own emotions/expectations to the side and make psychic space for him to step into. Listen with your heart, your mind, and your soul to what he may wish to communicate. Being able to commune with spirit requires a detached and unbiased listening process.
8. When you do get an image, a voice, a feeling, and your ego-mind tells you—and it will—"Oh, I'm just making this up," respond with, "Thank you for sharing, but I choose to believe this is real."
9. If you are open, you may experience a physical sensation like a soft touch on the cheek, a voice in your head, an uplifting in your heart, the sensation of a warm blanket being wrapped around you.
10. Be patient. If you don't sense any communication at first, don't give up. You may need some time to get used to the idea. Practice non-attachment. Your loved one may also need some practice in communicating with you on our physical plane. As I tell my clients, just because we invite someone to the party doesn't mean they will show up.
11. In the meantime, keep sending your love thoughts and keep holding the belief that he is there with you. According to your beliefs, be unto you.

Awomen/Amen. So be it. And so it is.

3

PSYCHIC BREAK-IN

The dawn light was slowly turning to daylight on this early Saturday morning. My day was booked solid with sessions for my North Vancouver clients. As a regular psychic reader at the *West Coast School of Mystic Arts, or "the psychic school" as I preferred to call it, I had been entrusted with my own key to the just-below-street-level office building.

Hauling my little wheeled black suitcase containing my psychic kit behind me, I negotiated the three concrete steps down to the metal-framed and glass-plated front door. As I approached the entrance, fumbling for the right key, nothing seemed particularly amiss, even when I saw the deadbolt protruding from the door, leaving it slightly ajar.

Another healer is already here expecting a client and has probably gone in to switch on the lights, I thought.

But when I got closer and saw a slim, twisted piece of metal lying ominously on the ground, I proceeded with caution. The piece of metal I recognized as part of the door lock. Gingerly opening the door, I realized too late that I should be using gloved hands. And maybe the burglars were still here . . . .

"Hello," I called out inanely as if robbers would rush out to greet me with "Oh, hi, Natasha. Coffee's on."

But there was just silence . . . . I listened. More silence.

As I peered around the reception area, still shrouded in the early morning shadows, nothing appeared disheveled or even mildly disturbed. Half-expecting to meet up with the intruders, I walked to the left into the Solar Room. Stacks of chairs were lined up against the faux-painted and moon-adorned walls. I turned and crept back along the corridor to the Lunar Room at the other end of the building, by-passing the closed office door. The same neat emptiness greeted me. Maybe they hadn't found what they were looking for or they had been disturbed in mid-burglary and fled. Or were they still here, hiding?

If I were really brave—or really stupid—I could go through the door at the rear into the kitchen where the lights for the entire floor were located and switch them all on. Then I wouldn't be fumbling around in the semi-darkness. I could also go into the rear corridor where the washroom was and see if anything was amiss there. But I wasn't that brave or that stupid. What should I do?

I opted to return to the reception desk and search for the telephone number of Elisabeth Hillier, another psychic and the person who, in the owner's absence, was in charge of the school.

Elisabeth's gentle manner and the vocal human contact, at least, were comforting. If the "perps" were still in hiding, at least someone would hear my screams. "Elisabeth, I hate to tell you this, but we've had a break-in."

There was a soft groan at the other end. "I had a feeling . . . ," she said.

After I gave her a brief description of the damage, she directed me to go to the office. As I approached the white door, for the first time I saw that the complete lock mechanism had been ripped out of the wooden panel, leaving a splintered, ragged, gaping hole.

"Look behind the door," she instructed. "On top of the filing cabinet, there should be a grey cash box."

"I don't see any cash box," I told her as I peered into the corner space.

Another small groan at the other end of the line.

"Was there a lot of cash in it?" I asked.

"No . . . maybe $50," she responded. "What about the laptop? Is that still there on top of the desk?"

I turned to face the desk. The office accessories all appeared to be in order, but the desk was bare.

"I don't see a laptop."

"Oh, god." Elisabeth sounded really upset now. "That had all *Kelly's database on it."

Yikes! I empathized. If I lost my computer with its database of my 4,000-plus clients, I too might consider it a bad day in hell.

"I'll call the police," she was saying.

"Just so you know, Elisabeth, my first client is coming at nine." Although I was overjoyed at the thought of not being alone in the building, it occurred to me that police sirens blaring and gun-toting officers surging into the room might not be conducive to a serene spiritual healing experience.

"I'll ask them to come as soon as possible," she said and hung up.

I walked back down the short hallway to the entrance and waited. When I glanced at my watch, I saw it was 8:50 a.m. Who would show first: the police, my client, or the robbers?

As I sat in the foyer, waiting in the hushed silence, I scanned the faux-painted mustard walls, the psychic development books, including my first book, *Aaagh! I Think I'm Psychic*, aligned on the glass shelves adorned with crystals, bookmarks, and other psychic accoutrements. On the other side were two rattan chairs for clients beside a small table with three magazines neatly laid on top. The reception desk was pristinely clean with pens, blotters, and business cards in place. It occurred to me how *undisturbed* everything was. The robbers had known what they were looking for and knew where to find it. *They have been here before*, I thought.

Then I stared at the glass-plated front door with its metal frame, this time seeing it from the inside, and realized how badly the handle and locks had been mangled, probably with a crow-bar. As I focused on that image, another image came to mind, that of two men, one tall and slim with brown hair, a Caucasian and the other shorter, stockier with black hair, a Hispanic. The taller boy/man was older, perhaps 23, more aggressive, the ringleader of the two, while the Hispanic younger man, I sensed, hadn't really wanted to be there.

I believe we all leave an energy residue wherever we go. Forensic scientists might call this residue dead skin, or epithelials, but the psychic energy I interpret as situation memory, an echo of our presence. When we are in a highly emotional or traumatized state, the energy residue is much stronger, almost palpable, for a psychic anyway. The front door was probably the spot where these burglars had been most scared, and the residue of their energy was still there, allowing me to "see" them as they broke in.

Good, I thought, I would be able to give the police this information—*if* they were the kind of police that respected psychics.

Pamela, my client, walked in the door before I could warn her not to touch the doorframe.

"Adds some excitement to my day," she responded when I informed her that the police would be here any minute and our reading might be interrupted.

"Good attitude!" I said. "And if you need even more excitement, you can take over my life for a while."

I had barely begun my preamble to Pamela's reading when, through the below-street-level windows, I saw the heavy black boots and telltale yellow-striped black pants of an RCMP officer pacing up and down, searching for the front door to the school. I excused myself from Pamela and went to find him.

Now that I had a protector, I showed him through the door to the kitchen and back rooms where I switched on the lights. He gave each area a cursory glance and frowned. "What do you do here anyway?"

Psychic school might scare him, I decided. "We teach spirituality, healing, meditation, psychic development."

The young blond-haired officer nodded, barely restraining a mocking grin.

"Are you going to dust for fingerprints or epithelials?" I asked, now a forensics expert after watching at least five episodes of *CSI*.

"Nah." He glanced at the destroyed metal frame. "Too many people have touched the door now."

More likely that lots of dead people would have to be lying about in our offices, I thought, before this police officer would bother fingerprinting. The theft of $50 and a laptop, I could feel, was merely interrupting his morning coffee hit.

"Actually," I told him, "I'm a psychic and I'm getting a sense of who they are."

"Oh, yeah?" He grinned again.

"Yes." I opted to ignore the skepticism as I know when I'm right and I was accustomed to disbelief. I described what I had felt and seen at the door. Then I added, "The taller man, he's used to doing break-ins. And they've both been here before. They knew exactly where to find what they were looking for."

The young policeman just nodded but I heard his thought. He couldn't wait to get back to the station and over coffee tell *this* story to his fellow officers. He followed me as I guided him to the Solar Room. Nothing there except my client who was patiently waiting, as if a police investigation were a normal precursor to a psychic reading.

"So," he asked quietly from behind me as we returned to the foyer, "could you give me the names and addresses of these two individuals?"

"No." I turned to face him, smiling. "You have to do some of the work, you know."

From the Rolodex, however, I was able to give him names and telephone numbers of other healers who were involved in the school. Then Elisabeth burst in the door.

"I saw them!" she announced to the officer.

"So did I! . . . But, oh . . . ," I paused, then wondered aloud, "but did you see them, or did you *see* them?" The officer, I could see, was confused. "I mean did you see them physically or psychically?" I amended.

Now he rolled his eyes while still trying to keep a straight face.

"Oh, no, I *saw* them." Elisabeth waved a hand toward the front of the building. "On the street last night." She turned to me. "I saw them not psychically but in the flesh." Then she looked earnestly at the officer, who was now pulling his notebook out of his back pocket and starting to write something down. At least he was taking Elisabeth seriously.

"There were two of them," Elisabeth said excitedly.

"What did they look like?" I asked, holding my breath. Had my vision been accurate? I knew and trusted what I saw, but maybe the energy of those two men was a leftover from another time or another break-in.

"One short, dark, Hispanic-looking and the other was taller, slimmer, with blond-brown hair."

The officer's pencil faltered as he realized Elisabeth was confirming what I had seen psychically.

"As I locked up last night," she continued, "I saw them driving slowly along the block in a big old green pick-up. I thought that something wasn't right then but I didn't think any more about it . . . until now of course. And . . ."

"Yes?" The police officer was listening now.

"Well," Elisabeth faltered. "I can't be positive but I think I saw them in here before, last week, pretending to look at the books, but really I sensed they were just snooping around."

Just as I thought. They had been here before.

"Allrightee then," the officer said, flipping his notebook shut, his body language trying not to betray his urge to flee. "We'll be in touch."

"Pretty silly," I commented to his retreating back, "for the robbers to break into a psychic school, don't you think?"

3 Shouldn't Psychics Know Better?

Dear Natasha,

I notice how many psychics make bad choices in their lives. Shouldn't they know better?

Dear Disillusioned,

This may come as a shock . . . and I don't mean to upset you . . . but . . . wait for it . . . yes, we psychics are *human*! Just like you, we are here on this planet to learn and evolve. We might be more attuned to a higher wisdom in some areas and we might be able to process problems more rapidly but, like you, we still have egos, face challenges, and feel feelings. Being able to see beyond ourselves is sometimes just as difficult for us as it is for our clients. Consequently, we buy non-winning lottery tickets, we have (very) bad days, we get confused, and, sorry, but . . . we also make bad choices.

Demystifying the myths and providing a reality check to those people with over-the-top expectations of psychics is just part of my mission as an inspirer of intuitive intelligence. My contribution to all the poor, misunderstood, ostracized, jeered-at, over-worked, underpaid psychics all over the planet is to put an end to the you're-psychic-so-you-should-know-better syndrome. So I *really* appreciate your question.

Even in this climate of spiritual awakening, the expectations of being a psychic *for* a psychic are still often unreasonable. Because psychic studies are not integral to the school curriculum, this lack of understanding is to be expected. But if the human species is to grow spiritually and creatively, we must first embrace our inherent intuitiveness by acknowledging our connection to our higher power. And we need to dispel the fear and ignorance that surround the word "psychic."

While I can appreciate why you would not want to accept spiritual counsel from a person whose life you consider to be imperfect, before you judge them too harshly, you might want to keep in mind another aspect of being psychic. We psychics are mostly—but not always—mouthpieces or mere channels for that higher wisdom. The words that spew forth in a reading are not coming necessarily *from* the psychic but *through* him or her. The information can also be messages that the psychic is sensing from your own mind, your spirit guides, the psychic's guides, or your God. So unless the psychic is projecting his or her own "stuff" onto you—which with some psychics can and does happen—your reading should have nothing to do with the psychic's personal life at the time. A good psychic will empower you to connect with your own truth.

If you believe that psychics possess superior knowledge, then the concept of their being beyond reproach is understandable. Remember that *all* humans come to the planet to learn lessons and particularly to love self. Psychic healers are not immune to those lessons. In fact, psychics often become psychic by going through major early childhood traumas. You could even say psychics *especially* need to go through the University of Life so they may be better qualified to counsel their clients compassionately. The higher our soul's evolution, the more challenging the tests are—just as in university. The "bad choices" that you are criticizing the psychic for failing to see might be the very lessons that particular psychic needs to learn at this time in his/her high-level evolutionary process. We are, therefore, just as vulnerable, sensitive, and emotionally impaired as all other people. So, yes, we *are* human and appreciate being treated as such.

Being a psychic isn't easy. The reasons we feel this job title can be a curse are outlined in my first book but the following are challenges that we also have to face:

- Psychics usually experience tougher-than-normal lives—in preparation for becoming healers.
- Psychics endure sometimes excruciating sensitivity to people, objects, atmospheres, places, and other vibrations.
- Psychics are often bombarded with demeaning insults, snickers, and verbal attacks from people who are afraid of the truth.
- Psychics are sometimes told that because we are doing God's work, we should offer our services for diddly-squat. But we psychics also like to pay our bills, eat, stay warm, live in houses, and put clothes on our backs. Yes, we're weird like that!
- Psychics are also sometimes told that we are doing the devil's work. We can't win.
- Psychics are expected to be permanently "on tap" and to know everything. While smart psychics are only tuned in during readings or when they otherwise *choose* to intuit for their own lives, being constantly psychically attuned would be akin to listening to 50 radio stations simultaneously—a recipe for insanity. My clients accept these boundaries. But hey, if someone wants to pay me a $20,000 retainer per month, I might consider being on a personal twenty-four-hour hotline. I still won't know everything, though.

- Psychics are often exhausted from healings because we feel and see all the pain our clients experience.
- Psychics are perceived as possessing special powers and are often isolated from "normal" people for that reason. In reality, all we humans are intuitive and could be psychic if we *listened* to energy, *trusted* what we heard, and then *acted* on that information.
- Psychic readings can, in my experience, consume four times the amount of energy as, for example, gardening. There are times when I would rather be in the garden.
- Psychics sometimes encounter wary reactions when they are doing perfectly ordinary things. So next time you find yourself in their line of sight in the supermarket, just remember that their eyes may not be boring into your soul but merely searching for the avocadoes.

Being psychic affords many blessings, of course, which I also detail in my first book. One of these blessings is that I am much more sensitive than . . . er . . . people who tell me "you should know better." And when I am facilitating healing and spiritual development with clients who graciously recognize the value of what I do, my work is extremely rewarding.

So, **dear Disillusioned**, the question I would have for you is: As the client, would you rather consult a psychic who has read about life experiences in a book or one who has emotionally undergone and understands the very same challenges that you are now facing? If you open your mind and allow your spiritual healers *not* to be perfect, all-knowing, angelic beings, you will be treated to a far deeper and more compassionate reading.

Perhaps the next time you think about saying, "You should know better" to a psychic, healer, psychologist, or inspirational speaker, you might remember that we all have egos, experience bad moments, get tired, feel emotional, make mistakes, or otherwise exhibit signs of the idiocy and frailty that we humans all share. Although our passion is to empower others, we are also just people in the human experience . . . just like you. And if you do forget, be happy in that moment that *you* cannot read *our* minds!

BACK FROM THE DEAD

Even the way I came into contact with Linda was a "meant-to-be." It was September and I was having fun at a Celestial Evening in Vancouver. Eight hundred men and women, all associated directly or indirectly with the film industry, swarmed through the two-tiered restaurant. I was there to read them, but the music and the noisy conversation were so loud that I had to shout my predictions at the clients sitting on the opposite side of my star-speckled tablecloth.

"I'm going to have a baby?" The 40-something man's shocked face frowned back at me.

"No." I smiled and strained to project my voice even louder. "You're going to meet a lady!"

"Oh," he responded, his frown transforming into a wide grin of relief.

When my contracted time of four hours was over, I started gathering up my psychic paraphernalia—crystals, cards, Kleenex—and putting them into my suitcase. After straining my voice against the hubbub for so long, and approaching psychic exhaustion, I was looking forward to some silence and a good long rest the following day.

I noticed a lady with short, blonde-gray curly hair hovering nearby. I felt something urgent in her energy. "Can I help you?" I offered.

"I have to see you," she whispered as I was blowing out the dripping non-drip candles.

"I'm finished for tonight . . . but okay," I agreed as if on autopilot. "I could see you tomorrow afternoon at your hotel." So much for rest. "Four o'clock?" I suggested.

"Thank you." She squeezed my hand as if I had just pulled her out of quicksand.

The next day on the dot of four, Veronica opened her hotel room door to me. I went straight for the hotel's standard round table in the corner, plugged in my tape deck, and lit the candle while Veronica's husband (I presumed) lay on the bed sleeping.

I took my client's hands, gave her my usual preamble, and then closed my eyes so I could tune in to her energy. Very quickly the urgency I had sensed in Veronica's body language the night before pushed itself front and center.

N: *Is there a lot of energy being expended on a child?*
V: *Yes.*
N: *Is it a son?*
V: *No, daughter.*
N: *It's serious? I feel a lot of illness.*
V: *Yes.*

Veronica almost breathed the last word out, full of relief that I was able to recognize her distress.

N: *How old is she now?*
V: *27.*
N: *I'm getting something that happened when she was 23.*
V: *She's been ill all her life but seriously for the last four years. So yes, 23 was a turning point . . . for the worse.*

As I focused on her daughter's energy, I slumped in my chair, suddenly overcome by exhaustion myself.

N: *I feel a lot of tiredness. Does she have CFS, Chronic Fatigue Syndrome, or something like that?*
V: *Yes!*

Veronica sat forward in her chair as if not wanting to miss a word I said. And despite the weariness I was empathizing in the daughter, I also felt a murmur of excitement about the daughter overcoming her condition, and my being able to help this woman through her pain.

N: *She has to make a decision . . . as if she's choosing between living and dying. There is a strong pull from another life, as if she has one foot in this life and another foot in the grave.*

V: (whispering as she glances over at her husband) *We've nearly lost her a few times.*

N: *Oh, this is interesting.* (I felt a huge pull on her daughter's energy like a giant magnet to somewhere out in the ether.) *Something happened in another life that's keeping her partially stuck there. A trauma. That's why she's ill—because half her energy is somewhere else. She needs to decide soon whether she wants to live or die. I sense, though, that she has already made that decision. I see her getting better—very slowly, but she will recover, three steps forward, two back.*

V: (letting out a long sigh of relief) *What can we do?*

N: *She may need some past-life work. If I could read her personally, I would be able to sense more clearly what's holding her back.*

An hour later as Veronica unplugged my tape deck and I placed my psychic tools back in the case, she said, "Maybe you could come to Kelowna."

"Tell you what. If you can get, oh . . . twenty people together for readings, I'll fly up there," I offered as I strolled toward the door.

"Don't be surprised if you get a call," a man's voice warned. I turned and saw that the "sleeping" man was now sitting upright, his light-framed glasses perched on his nose, a newspaper on his lap.

"My husband, David," Veronica grinned sheepishly.

"Like you just said," he continued, "she's a tigress when it comes to her children." His lips barely curled up in a smile. As I suspected, he had been listening to every word.

Ten days later Veronica called. "Well, I've got twenty people," she announced breathlessly, as if she'd just run back from enrolling the last one. "When can you come?"

"You are a tigress, aren't you?" We both chuckled.

Three weeks later, my friend Sarah was giving me a big hug at Kelowna airport's arrival hall. The next day she dropped me off in front of Veronica's house to begin my three-day psychic-reading marathon and, hopefully, to help Linda.

When I first laid eyes on Linda, what I had seen in her mother's reading all made sense. As she leaned her tall skinny frame against Veronica so she wouldn't keel over, I was shocked at how her shiny, plasticky, yellow-white skin clung to her slight body. Her brown eyes had no life in them, as if she were already dead. *Most of her spirit has blown this popsicle stand a long time ago*, I thought. *God help me to help her,*

I silently prayed, *but she has to be willing.* After all, you can't make a person want to live or even want to change.

I was ushered into a cozy guest room that offered the illusion of a private hushed little world, perfect for readings. Linda was my fourth reading of the day. Expressionless, she sat gingerly in the chair across from me and hunched over the square card table. She seemed barely able to support herself; I wanted to lean over and prop her up. *God, I hope she doesn't die on me while I'm doing the reading,* I thought. I held her delicately lined, clammy hands in mine. Then the movie started rolling in the center of her palm.

N: *I see you wearing a long black dress with a white hat and long white apron, in France, probably in the 1600 or 1700s. You're working in your father's inn. I believe it's during the time of the battle between the Huguenots and the . . . Catholics?* (My knowledge of French history isn't impressive.) *You are waiting . . . for your beau to come.* (I saw an ardent young man, full of bravado, heroism, and love for the young woman that she was.) *You're very, very in love with him. He is your soul mate, a great, great love. There's a rebellion, an ongoing battle in which he is a leader. He's a swashbuckler type who loves the adventure of it all. He has taken a great risk to come to the inn to see you. As you stand whispering on the upstairs gallery in the dark, a man comes out of the shadows and . . . oh . . . oh . . . no . . .* (as I relayed this information to her, I felt her overwhelming and complete pain) *. . . kills your lover and soul mate . . . . He stabs him right in the heart.* (I clutched my hand over my heart feeling the physical blow her lover felt.) *You watch in horror, helpless.*

We sat there in silence, suddenly aware of the stillness of the room. As I allowed the huge wave of sadness to pass through me and leave my body, I reminded myself to breathe again. Release, release, release.

N: *Not long after this incident, you die of a broken heart.*

A small sound came out of Linda's mouth. Was it recognition and empathy for this tragic woman who might have been her in a past life, or an expression of her present pain? I didn't want to tax her already waning energy by asking questions.

N: *The loss of your soul mate is bad enough, but you also seem to be carrying the guilt for his demise because you think you gave his arrival away to the enemy.*

Linda suddenly looked up, her eyes pleading. But pleading for what? I wondered. Redemption?

N: *It wasn't your fault.* (Holding back my own tears, I gave her hand a very gentle squeeze, afraid that it could easily break.) *He got a little careless.*

I glanced up at Linda to see if this information made any sense to her. But now nothing in her cadaverous face so much as twitched with recognition.

N: *Part of you is still stuck in that time. If I were to go back to that inn, if it's still standing, I would see you reverberating from the trauma, pacing up and down along that gallery. You're haunting the place. Part of you is a ghost.*

I paused and took a gulp of water. Still no response from Linda.

N: *I understand that you really miss your soul mate, but he has not incarnated this time. You're aching to be with him and you don't really want to be here at all. It's your decision whether you get well or not. But you do need to stay in this life and do the work. He's encouraging you to live and reminding you that you are indeed soul mates. He'll be waiting for you when you leave this life—but only at the right time. He also wants you to know that he is always with you in spirit.*

I paused again as I let her absorb the information. She didn't even blink, so I carried on undeterred. It was important that she hear this.

N: *I believe that, on a subconscious level, you have already chosen to stay, and once you decide to commit on the conscious level, you will get better physically. It will be a gradual improvement, but you will heal. It would benefit you greatly to see a past-life regressionist to help you bring these memories to consciousness so that you can heal the part of you that's stuck and reclaim that part of your soul.*

L: *Do you know someone who can do that?*

Until then, there had not been a flicker of a smile, or a nod or a tear, from Linda. So when she spoke, I nearly jumped.

N: *Uh . . . uh . . . not in Kelowna . . . . But I will find someone.*

This I said with absolute conviction, not having a clue how I was going to locate a professional in the next twenty-four hours to whom I could entrust the fragile Linda. I could have done the past-life regression myself, but I wasn't familiar with this depth of trauma and my first rule is "Do no harm." I gave the task of finding the right healer over to the Universe.

Later that day, Sarah invited me to go with her to a Wellness Fair. As soon as we walked into the monster exhibition hall, I knew this was where I would find the person who would help Linda heal her split soul. Sarah and I separated to explore the various exhibits of vitamins, herbs, aromatherapies, and self-help books. Then, as I came to the center of the hall, I was delighted to see the next aisle consisted of a row of tables presided over by a variety of psychics, spiritual healers, aura readers, and other healing practitioners busy chatting to potential clients and handing out brochures. I stopped at the first table to investigate their list of services. The words on the pale green brochure leapt off the page at me: "Soul Retrieval." As I read the description of the process, I gasped. It was exactly what Linda needed. As I moved from table to table, I saw that each practitioner was advertising soul retrieval. In all my years of metaphysical learning, I had never even heard the term. Yet here, strangely, in this small town, a variety of psychics, healers, and other wellness-practitioners had gathered, all of whom were apparently experts on reclaiming lost souls—just when I needed this service.

Which one to pick for Linda? I stood in the middle of the tables, closed my eyes, and asked for guidance. When I opened them, I saw the sign. A large banner on the last table at the end of the row read: "Past Life Traumas with a Psychological Approach." And that's what drew me to RB's table. I warmed to his gentle, down-to-earth manner as I relayed Linda's past life history to him. "Do you think you can help her?" I asked.

"It may take a few sessions but if, as you say, she has decided to get well, then yes." I also trusted that with his psychology background, he would at least do my client no harm. He was, I knew, the one.

§

That was October. The following January I returned to Kelowna to do more readings and facilitate two workshops. Linda, to my surprise, wanted an updated reading. What was even more astounding was Linda herself.

She opened the door to greet me, and I was gobsmacked. Gone was the corpse-like pallor. Those previously dull brown eyes had life in them, that white, white skin had taken on a pinkish hue, and she was chatting! Not just talking, but chatting with a sparkle in her voice.

Linda's second reading confirmed what I saw in her body. Her spirit had finally surrendered to being here now. The past life issue did not show itself at all. Usually if I don't see an issue, either I am not meant to see it or the problem doesn't exist. What her latest reading did indicate was a lot of progress—more like a normal reading, whatever normal is. I described what I envisioned her new life to be: moving out of her parents' home, a new residence, independence, and oh, yes, a new love. Her spirit had definitely decided to live.

She was back from the dead.

4 What Is Soul Retrieval?

Dear Natasha,

I was recently told that I need to do some soul-retrieval work. What does that mean exactly?

Dear Soul-Retriever,

Just as our computers require a regular defragging to clean out old files and reconcile new data, many of us need to regularly clear out our mental and emotional garbage. Otherwise, consciously or unconsciously, we give away our power to fear, a memory of fear, or guilt. This leaking of energy drains us of our inherent power and the subsequent dis-ease will manifest in our current experience as "stuckness," phobias, illness, overwhelming fatigue, depression, or other seemingly inexplicable symptoms.

Soul retrieval is based on the belief that a piece of our soul is trapped in a past life because of unresolved trauma there. A similar dynamic occurs when we don't totally process the psychological injuries we encounter in our present lives: our psyches get "stuck," as if time had stopped at the moment of the trauma. Because we usually have waking memories of these injuries in the present life, it is relatively easy for us to access the trauma that needs to be healed.

But when the trauma is buried in a past life, accessing and healing it becomes more challenging. What presents then is akin to a constant fretting, conscious or unconscious, about something precious we have left behind.

In each lifetime, we experience our lives through the lens of different spirits or personalities. Each spirit is just one aspect of our soul. Like the many prisms of a crystal, all those soul aspects or spirits make up the entirety of our soul. And the soul is eternal and forever evolving.

When an aspect of our soul chooses to be born again—in the form of a new spirit—into the physical plane, we agree to experience life's lessons through that spirit which is then housed in a physical body. Our spirit reports back to our souls the information we gather through our learning here on earth. However, if a piece of our soul—or one of our spirits from a former life—did not find peace at the end of that life and did not heal, that spirit will stay attached to that former life's time and place. When the spirit is ready to become unstuck, that piece of our soul will seek release through healing.

This pattern also holds true for trauma experienced in our current lives. If we do not "finish" and resolve our traumas, the pain can be easily triggered by people or events and we can remain stuck in it.

While digging into past lives is effective, we don't always have to go that far back to revisit the issue. After all, in any given moment we are the sum total of all our experiences, past and present. If we heal the now and refresh our perceptions, then, like a reverse domino effect, we can also heal our past and recalibrate our present.

So, **dear Soul-Retriever**, soul retrieval is the process of healing and reclaiming the lost part of your soul. But because this pain is often so deeply buried, we frequently require outside assistance to access the root cause. Various healing modalities are available including hypnotherapy, past-life regression, EFT (Emotional Freedom Technique), NLP (Neuro-Linguistic Programming), and trauma counseling. If you are going to explore your past lives, trust your intuition to guide you to the best modality and practitioner for you. Only you will know when, and with whom, you are ready to restore that piece of your psyche and be totally empowered and whole once again.

ONCE UPON A SOUL-MATE DAY

It was a Wednesday and just another dreary October day. The gray skies of a British Columbia fall had closed in around my suburban house like a dark cave, and, of course, it was raining. The rain seemed endless but then, I had to remind myself, I *did* live in a rain forest. Still, this particular kind of drizzle seeped into my bones and made my spirit feel soggy.

I reviewed my agenda for the day—two appointments for psychic readings, and, as always, the never-ending household chores like laundering, baking cookies, picking up the kids from school, and driving them to their various activities. The usual. Or so I thought.

As I waited for my first client, Suzi, to arrive, I did my pre-reading rituals: checked the cleanliness of the bathroom, primped the cushions in my living room, put on the kettle for tea, laid out the blue-moon-and-star teacups, and lighted the candles and incense in my "reading" room. I was grateful to be in my own home and not to have to travel off-coast to do my work today.

Suzi had come to me a few months previously at the bookstore in Vancouver where I did my bi-monthly psychic sessions. Today, the pretty 35-year-old had decided to travel all the way from the city, a forty-minute ferry ride followed by an additional hour's drive through the countryside. For me, the boat trip between this long peninsula where I lived and the mainland was like a mini-cruise, sailing through the serenity of the islands and the beautiful mountain scenery, so I knew that despite the inclement weather, the journey would be a pleasant one for her. I should be flattered that my client had chosen to come all this way to see me, but it was more likely that she just couldn't wait for my next session in the city bookstore. Or perhaps she needed a brief respite from the noisy chaos of the metropolis, especially on a day like today. I could relate.

The phone rang. Roberta's husky voice was unmistakable. She was a client from the west side of Vancouver.

"Natasha!" She sounded excited. "You were right!"

I furiously tried to recall our last reading. *What had I told her? Right about what? Help!*

"I've met him. Just like you said!"

Thank god. But who?

"Remember you told me that I wasn't to leave town because if I did I would never find my soul mate?"

I did? "Vaguely. Yes."

"Well, business at my company was so bad that I seriously considered getting the hell out of Dodge, but Laura reminded me of what you said and told me to stay." Laura, my long-time girlfriend, had introduced me to Roberta and suggested she have a reading with me. "Well, that winter," Roberta continued, now on a roll, "I went skiing and literally bumped into him on the mountain. The connection was amazing. We had a wonderful time. He took my phone number. Then I never heard from him again."

"Oh, no." *Then why did she sound so full of joy?*

I knew there was more, and Roberta didn't need any prompting. "Remember you told me we would meet, but it would be difficult getting together in the beginning?"

"I did?"

"Yes, Natasha, you did."

"So what happened?" I was now dying to hear the outcome of this one. So many soul-mate stories in my world end badly.

"Well, then Betty urged me to call him." I remembered Betty, another friend of Laura's. She would urge anybody to do anything. I had only met her once but I wouldn't want to argue with this Amazonian fitness trainer. "At first," Roberta continued, "I wasn't going to because . . . well . . . you know."

"Oh, yes, I know." *Don't chase the man* was my philosophy, though I have been known—on more than one occasion—to cave.

"So finally I did call him." Roberta sounded as if she were going to end the narrative there, but I realized she was merely coming up for air.

"And?"

"He was *so* happy to hear from me," she exclaimed, the smile in her voice.

Phew!

"He told me he was glad I had called because he had lost my number and couldn't remember the name of the company I worked for. He'd been trying to figure a way of finding me. Anyway, we've been seeing each other ever since and we're really happy."

"I'm so happy for you, Roberta," I said, happy for me, too. When a soul mate I have predicted actually arrives in my client's life, I breathe a huge sigh of relief. Because if they don't manifest immediately, I never hear the end of it.

"You also told me he was from across the border. He lives in Tacoma, and we're talking about me moving down there."

"Wow! That's great."

The line fell silent. Her excitement now expended, Roberta added, "I just thought I would share that with you." This woman, who presented a tough exterior, sounded a little shy about having gushed so unabashedly.

"Well, thank you, Roberta," I responded, my turn to be enthusiastic. "I love to hear back from my clients and find out what actually manifested. I don't tell people what they want to hear just to make them feel good, you know. If we just keep the faith, most of the time what I see does show up eventually."

"Faith is not my strong point." Roberta grunted but the joy in her voice brimmed over.

Just then, *Bear, our huge black lab-husky, moved to the front door, his large tail waving, creating its own vortex. Then I heard a *clump, clump* of feet on the porch.

"Roberta, sorry, I have to go. My client's here. But stay in touch. And be happy."

"I will," she chuckled. "I'll get another reading from you some time."

"Yes, maybe," I responded, knowing that she wouldn't need me to guide her future now.

As Suzi stepped into my hallway, she emitted a skittish, nervous energy that combined with a mild sense of relief at having survived the journey. Like a dog coming out of a pond, she shook the rain off her trademark smart black city attire. "Good directions," she beamed at me, her fine straight black hair framing a petite face. "I didn't get lost once."

"Yes, the route sounds long and complicated but it isn't really," I said, taking her wet jacket and hanging it close to the heater. *Kind of like life,* I thought. *We just need directions along the way. I guess that's what I'm here for.*

As we started the session with Suzi's delicate hands outstretched, I immediately sensed the presence of a male energy. He seemed a little faint to me, which could mean he was either emotionally distant or physically far away. I described what I saw to Suzi. Something struck me as familiar about him.

She smiled conspiratorially. "You told me about him the last time, Natasha. You said he was my soul mate and I actually have met him in the way you described."

You did? Hmmm? If only I could remember my prediction.

"There was no mistaking him," Suzi continued. "He told me the sports he's into. They're the ones you described. And his personality, his family, everything was just as you told me. It was quite amazing."

Was? "But you're not together yet?"

"Well, you also told me that we would meet and talk but not get together immediately. He has to stay in Kamloops on a job contract and won't be back until March." Suzi stared into her upturned palms as if she might see the answer there herself. "So you still see him, do you?" she asked as I studied the lines in her hands.

"Oh, yes. I still get a feeling of the two of you dancing around each other, but when the feelings are that strong, that dance is pretty normal. If you think about it, when we're not used to that level of emotion and the love suddenly arrives, many of us, especially men, tend to go into a spiral. Then we can behave in uncharacteristic ways."

"Makes sense," Suzi said quietly. Despite her natural edginess, she seemed to be taking the situation calmly—unlike some of my clients. She just smiled knowingly.

I was puzzled by her reaction. I know how painful it can be to meet your soul mate and then have to sit and wait. *Torturous* is actually the word that comes to mind.

"No, it's okay," she said, sensing my concern. "I just know we're going to be together. And in some ways I still have to get myself prepared and be ready for him."

"*Exactly!*" I exclaimed, thrilled that this young woman actually understood the concept of like attracts like. "Would you *please* convey that to my other clients who can't seem to grasp that thinking? We need to meet our soul mates on their level and then make a space for them in our lives that they can step into. If we're not ready, it falls apart. And if there's no space, they can't stay. They leave and will have to return when we are ready to make the space for them."

While the rest of the session was merely a more detailed version of my predictions two months earlier, it re-confirmed her career direction and an imminent house purchase followed by the move into her first home. Those events were all still out there in the ether, waiting to manifest, and that was okay with her. Apparently Suzi just needed the reassurance that my previous predictions were still potentials in her future.

"Whatever will be, already is," I reminded her, "and what is yours will come to you."

"Yes, I have to remember that," she said, nodding and mentally filing the words away in her mantra list.

"Sometimes," I added, "even when we know, we like to be reassured that what we know is what we know, if you know what I mean—especially when it comes to soul mates."

I enjoyed Suzi's company and would have invited her to stay for lunch, but another client of mine needed an urgent session. Teresa had called the previous night also from Vancouver in a state of panic and needed to talk to me . . . about her soul mate. She would be arriving soon.

Suzi seemed quite content to take her tape and drive off into the countryside, ruminating over her reading and relaxing before she had to get back on the ferry and once more deal with the busy city. "Though there wasn't much new in the reading," she told me, sliding her arms into a slightly drier jacket, "I got what I came for."

"Good. What was that?" I asked, though I already knew.

"Validation."

As I watched her pick her way down my path to her car, I noticed that some of her prior nervousness had dissipated and her aura now emanated a deeper sense of serenity.

I just had time to gulp down some homemade vegetable soup before Bear was, once again, panting expectantly at the front door. The knocking this time was more urgent. I braced myself against the whirlwind of emotion that would be coming into the house.

"Hi, Teresa," I said, pulling the door wide to allow her big spirit to enter.

As she stepped inside, I attempted a grin but I could feel all the tension hunched in her shoulders. Seeing she was on the verge of an emotional explosion, I shielded myself psychically against the force of her confusion. She didn't know whether to burst out crying, scream, hug me, explode in anger, or nail me to the wall and demand to know why the hell what I had told her in the previous reading hadn't yet manifested. Sometimes it's hard being the messenger.

When I offered Teresa a cup of green tea, she brusquely shook her head. Uninvited, she stomped ahead of me, proceeding straight to my reading room as if to say, *Let's get on with it!* I followed her in, a glass of water in my hand.

I started to tune in, but Teresa didn't want to wait for my words of wisdom.

"I have to tell you something," she sputtered, still with an earnest smile on her face. "I'm so mad at you that I've thrown the previous tapes away."

We both burst out laughing. I loved Teresa for her honesty. Like me, she's a Taurus, blonde-haired, blue eyed, and, also like me, passionate and stubborn. We understood each other.

"So you don't believe what I told you about B-Man and you getting together in the fall?"

"Oh . . . ." She slumped back into the chair. Her body seemed to hiss as if she were a hot air balloon whose plug had been pulled leaving her to fall, deflated, to the ground. "You still think that's going to happen?" The small childish plea in her voice held within it the ember of hope that she was urging me to reignite. Her whole body language screamed, *Please just say Yes!* "I love that man so much," Teresa almost cried. She laid her hand on her heart as if to heal it and glanced out my window at the lush green forest. "I know it's crazy," she continued. "We haven't spent any time together, yet I can feel him in my heart. I feel him. I feel where he is, feel him when he's thinking about me."

"Oh, I know, I know," I commiserated, sounding like Sybil from *Fawlty Towers.* I did know all about being able to feel a soul mate even when that person was on the other side of the world. It wasn't the physical presence that connected us. So many people didn't get that. "But Teresa," I took her hands in mine, "he can't come into your life until you've made space for him. You are still married, remember?"

"I know, I know." She sat back in her chair, not wanting to be reminded. "But what's his problem? That's just a minor detail." We both laughed then.

"I think that's what's keeping him away from you," I told her, peering into her palms, waiting to see the psychic film clips that would give me the information. The moving images always told me what was about to transpire in the person's life. "I sense that he doesn't want to approach you because he doesn't know that you're so unhappy. He doesn't know that you're thinking of leaving your husband. But you need to clear up your marriage and complete that before you go running into the arms of another."

Teresa's eyes searched mine. "I hate you," she barked. I knew she didn't really mean that but she didn't want to hear the truth either.

"Not only for your own self-respect, but just to keep the lines clear," I added.

"But you still think it's going to happen?" she asked yet again. How badly she wanted to hang onto this vision and be right about her own feelings.

"How many times do I have to tell you? Nothing has changed." I got weary of repeating myself with some of my clients. "It's *you* who doesn't have faith."

She sank back in the high-backed wooden chair, her aura vibrating chaotically.

"Why would you think it's *not* going to happen?" I asked.

Though I already knew the answer to that, I wanted her to think about it and say the words: she did not dare believe that she could actually be happy. At the same time, she needed to believe my predictions would manifest. It was a conflict. For a moment, she pondered what I had said.

"Why won't you believe?" I asked again.

"Because there have been no signs from him." The tears threatened to break loose again. "But you know something?" she said, her voice breaking. "When I bump into B-Man at the grocery store, I catch him giving me sidelong glances. He waves every time he goes by in his car. And we're always bumping into one another at the gas station. But how do I know he likes me?"

I laughed then.

Teresa tilted her head to one side, hurt and puzzled. "This isn't funny, Natasha. Why are you laughing?"

"Because all the things you've just told me *are* signs!"

Teresa was still frowning, staring down at her palms as my previous client had done, searching for guarantees of happiness.

"Teresa, if I were to ask you, 'Will you be with him?' what would you answer me?"

"I don't know," she exclaimed. "You're the psychic!"

I chose to ignore that last comment. My job is to empower my clients to connect with and trust their own inner voices. I am not a fortune-teller. My intention is to make my clients excavate their own truth.

"You *do* know." I squeezed her hands. "You do."

She lifted her head, almost surprised. Her face broke into a beam of joy. "Yesss!" she said definitively. "He's mine. I see myself getting married to him. You know, Natasha, I had this vision . . . even before I knew who he was."

"So there's your answer. You *do* know. We all know the truth inside if we just trust it."

Once Teresa finally relaxed about her soul mate, I was able to move on to guide her through the morass of her separation and the beginning of a new life, which on her subconscious level she had already planned.

"Your husband already knows that you're planning on separating?" It was more of a statement than a question on my part.

"No!"

"I think he does know. He may be in denial. But you need to tell him soon."

"I'm scared. I don't have a job. Will he get violent?"

"No, I don't see that, and if I did, I would tell you to get the hell out of there." I paused to go deeper. "You're going to be working in the realty world and you'll do well at it. The money's good."

Teresa nodded. "I used to work as a mortgage broker and I was thinking about applying to a couple of the local companies."

"Just be gentle with your husband," I said. "After all, he is also one of your soul mates."

Teresa harrumphed.

"Just speak your truth, but empower him as you do it. Give him a path, a way of seeing that this separation is the best thing that could happen to him. I don't see him as the type that would go for counseling, which is too bad. It's always the people who really need counseling who refuse to go."

Teresa nodded. She was calmer now, somewhat mollified.

"So take care of your work and family first. And then when you are free, I see B-Man, your soul mate, approaching you in the fall. You're walking in the park near your house with your dog. Your head is down as if you're trying to avoid him. You're mad at him about something. And, oh, Teresa, what a surprise!" I smiled at her then.

"What?" She was giggling now.

"You, of all people, are stubbornly determined not to acknowledge him. But he is chasing you and calling out your name and wants to get your attention."

She laughed out loud, not refuting my vision of her stubborn and passionate nature.

"You *will* be together," I reassured her. "It won't be a clear path but it will happen and when it does you will be very happy."

"You better be right." Teresa stared at me sternly, a twinkle in her eye.

God help me if I'm not, I thought but I responded with "Thanks for the vote of confidence."

After Teresa left and before I had to leap into the car to pick up my stepchildren, I relaxed on the couch with a cup of tea. I realized then that this day was anything but ordinary. This day was Soul-Mate Day.

My own romantic soul mate had been physically absent in my life for twenty years, yet I was still connected to him on a heart level. That love would never die. But now, today, I was in a committed relationship with a wonderful man, another soul mate, and his three special children. And yes, soul mates are plural, not singular. Maybe the answer to the eternal soul-mate question is to treat everyone in our lives as preciously as that romantic ideal. Like the song says, *If you can't be with the one you love, love the one you're with.* I would add: Love everyone you're with.

Just before I climbed into my car, I decided it's all about being in the present and accepting what—and who—is in our lives today. If we practiced love in that way, when the ideal romantic soul mate finally shows up, we wouldn't be so terrified of allowing ourselves to be loved so intensely. We would be more conscious that everyone in our lives is, indeed, our soul mate . . . if we make it so. And if we truly love our authentic selves and truly love others, and if like attracts like, then doesn't it make sense that we would then attract true love?

§

A few weeks later Teresa called me, excitement in her voice. "Natasha, I got the job as a mortgage broker, and Tony's being good so far. Your advice really helped me break it to him."

Phew! "So you were right, Natasha."

It's never about being right. For me, it's about people living their truth and being in their power. We can only be empowered through a willingness to love and be loved, to be soul mates for each other.

5 When Will I Meet My Soul Mate?

Dear Natasha,

When will I meet my soul mate?

Dear Soul-Mate Seeker,

When clients ask me this question, the conversation goes like this:

Client:	When will I meet my soul mate?
Natasha:	When you are ready.
Client:	When will I know that I'm ready?
Natasha:	When you have met your soul mate.
Client:	Huh?

Let me explain.

Because soul mates can be such powerful reflections of our deepest essence and of how we love or don't love ourselves, these intense relationships can be all-consuming and terrifying. So be careful what you wish for because meeting the soul mate is not for the faint of heart. You have to be ready.

Sometimes my clients *meet* their soul mates but don't end up *being* with them. This path can depend on your soul agreement, the contract you made with your own soul before you were born. If you or your soul mate made an agreement to do other work on the planet—as in find the cure for cancer—then these big loves can distract us from our mission. Sometimes our soul mates will appear later in life, once we are on track with our primary goals.

Soul mates can often sideswipe you, suddenly appearing when you're *not* looking. The power of one of these encounters can be like a monster tidal wave thundering down on an innocent child while she's making sandcastles on a beach with her back to the ocean. When it's too late to run, the innocent knows she stands no chance. It's gonna get her. The wave predictably throws her off balance. She almost drowns in all that foaming tumbling emotion, the joy as well as the fear of the overwhelming magnitude of the wave. Soul-mate love brings the duality of heart-bursting joy and terror at the thought of losing the hard-won happiness. When she finally comes up for air, and she feels that she can absorb some of this wave of emotion, she might stand on her own two feet only to find that the person for whom she felt all this overwhelming love is so terrified that he himself has run for the hills.

Her worst fears have come true, and she is left, once again, alone on the beach with cold, salty water lapping around her limp body, stinging with agonizing regularity the empty space in her chest that is the open, bloody wound where her heart used to beat. She is wondering, "What was that?"

And although her heart has been ripped out, she still loves that person, even though her love has nowhere to be expressed or accepted. That force of nature just sits in her empty, bleeding, wounded chest, and she just has to learn to live with it. Eventually she will carry on, but she will never ever love like that again because no one else can touch her or make her feel that way. Every romance that follows is like a mere shadow of the intense love she has known, and she can only love like a piece of cardboard, a flat, two-dimensional love. "'Tis better to have loved and lost / Than never to have loved at all"—or so Alfred Lord Tennyson wrote. She can never, ever forget, not for one day, not for one moment, how it felt to feel, just to feel, the magnitude of that love.

So, **dear Soul-Mate Seeker**, do you still want to meet your soul mate? Okay, brave soul. First, let me give you some survival tips!

First Law of Attraction: Get ready. Recognize your inner truth by the romantic results you experience in your life. You might *feel* ready to plunge into a new relationship in your ego-conscious mind, yet on the subconscious level, a block may be preventing a relationship from happening. Perhaps you do not love yourself enough, perhaps you're afraid of getting hurt again, perhaps you're still healing from a past hurt, or perhaps you're too busy in your work where it's emotionally safer to invest your energy. Whatever the reason for the avoidance, the result is the same. No soul mate.

As if he were already in your life, visualize being happily in love with your soul mate. Then surrender to your higher power, relax, and be yourself. Let your angels worry about the details and cherish yourself the way you want your soul mate to cherish you so when he does show up, you are not unprepared but ready, willing, and able to be loved. Know this: On the deepest level, loving yourself the way your soul mate will love you melts all the blocks and will attract your soul mate to you.

Second Law of Attraction: Like attracts like, that is, your vibration has to be the same as or complementary to your prospective mate's in order for the two of you to meet. Be your authentic self and then you will attract the like or complementary energy that can be your true love.

Third Law of Attraction: Soul-mate agreements are magnetic. Sometimes the work of the soul-mate relationship can be our life purpose and part of the soul agreement we made before we were born into this lifetime. When the soul-mate relationship arrives and we feel as though we have no control over it, we are in fact channeling love as part of that agreement. As it says in *The Book of Runes*, "We do not love, but love loves through us." The challenges that arise in being able to love our soul mates unconditionally are essentially motivating us to do our life's work, which is to love ourselves at that high level. (Just to be clear, unconditional love does *not* include tolerating any kind of abuse.) And remember: What is yours will come to you.

In closing, do not use the absence of a soul mate in your life as an excuse to berate yourself. The time will come when you are truly ready. Then you won't even have to think about how to meet your soul mate because—like a force of nature—he will be irresistibly magnetized to the beautiful, self-loving essence you are.

DOG OR MIRACLE?

The Solar Room with its misty blue suns, moons, and stars scattered around the yellow, faux-painted walls offered some serenity after a taxing day of psychic readings. This area of the healing school is partially below street level, and the narrow windows that run along the top of the wall were now all as black as the night outside. I knew I probably shouldn't be alone in a building that had recently been broken into twice, but then—as now—I believed in the miracle protection of the white light and had faith that, wherever I was, the angels would watch over me.

I was just beginning to pack up the psychic accoutrements from my reading table when a "shoosh" sound startled me—was it the front door opening? When I peeked into the reception area, a very, very pregnant woman was bustling through the door. She beamed at me. "Hi, Natasha," she said, a familiar tone in her greeting and a big smile on her face.

"Oh. Do you have an appointment?"

"Yes, with you. Sheena Van Ritter. At six. Didn't they tell you?"

"No . . . but it's okay. Come on in." I locked the front door behind her. She would definitely be my last reading of the day. "Have I read you before, Sheena?" I asked as I followed her into the Solar Room.

She stopped dead, turned around, and stared at me, shocked. "Well, yeah, Natasha. Don't you remember?" I must have appeared to be having a blonde moment, and somehow I knew that the fetal protrusion of her stomach should be triggering a response from my mental client files. "Last year," she said. "It wasn't so much a reading. More like a forty-five minute argument about me having another baby!"

"Oh, yes, *now* I remember!"

Normally I never forget a face so I can only suppose that eight months of pregnancy had changed Sheena's physiognomy. In defense of my own memory, when I get a run of six readings in a day, I spend most of the time peering into fleshy palms and not studying facial features.

Now it was all coming back to me.

§

Sheena had arrived just after my lunch break. It was summer and the room at the back of the metaphysical bookstore where I did my readings was small, hot, and stuffy. The store's owner had attempted to turn the cramped space into a serene and comfy space conducive to psychic readings by draping floaty material over the chipped walls and placing candles, crystals, and a plant on a small table that she had covered with brown velvet, but as the saying goes, you can't make a silk purse out of sow's ear. The chairs were wooden and without cushions, uncompromising, especially after hours of readings. The open window allowed in a mildly forgiving breeze, but then my clients and I were subjected to the noise of monster trucks unloading in the alley behind with their squealing brakes, clanging car doors, whooshing hydraulics, the rat-tat-tat of roll-up doors snapping open, and the carbon dioxide-laden fumes. Often I was forced to choose between breathing—window open—or letting my clients actually hear their readings—window closed. The only feature to commend the space was that it was private.

Sheena sat down and instantly leaned forward as if to say, "I'm ready. Tell it all." With her brown-blonde curly hair, high cheekbones, and intense blue eyes, she looked Finnish or at least from one of the Nordic races, but she told me her heritage was Dutch. Close. In my experience, the people of the Netherlands and their descendants are an earthy, sturdy bunch. She would need those qualities.

As I took her hands in mine, I gave her my preamble. "Everything I see is a manifestation of what you are holding in your consciousness on some level today. What I say is only a potential for the future and not necessarily what will actually manifest."

Sheena nodded as if to say, "I can handle that."

"There's a question about career?" I started.

"Always," she said.

"And something about your husband's career is also changing?"

She shrugged and grinned wryly. "He's not working now so any change in the career department would be good."

"Does his name begin with J? John, something like that?"

"Yes, John. Very good," she said, leaning further in.

"He's got back trouble but it's going to get better. And he will be returning to work but in a different capacity. More on a consultancy level."

Sheena liked that. "That would be good," she said.

"There is also a change for you in career . . . but there's something . . . oh . . . ?

"What is it?" She searched my eyes, concerned.

I didn't know how old Sheena was. I guessed she must be in her forties, probably at or near the end of her child-bearing days. "You're going to have a baby," I announced.

It was as if I had shot a four-thousand-volt shock through her body. She shuddered with the impact of my words then quickly composed herself again and snorted. "That's impossible! I've had my tubes tied."

"Really? . . . Really?" Then what was I seeing? "A baby would *be impossible then, wouldn't it?" I said. I was no expert on the workings of the reproductive organs, although I had twice predicted men with vasectomies having more children, and much to the chagrin of one of them, the pregnancy actually happened. The other man, after my reading, had his vasectomy re-checked, apparently just in the nick of time—'scuse the pun. He and the doctor discovered that it hadn't "taken" and my client was compelled to have the procedure redone.*

However, I had never heard of a woman with her tubes tied being able to have babies. So this didn't make sense. But I was seeing and feeling a baby coming through Sheena.

"You're probably seeing my dog," Sheena suggested.

"Hmm . . . no . . . . Actually . . . I'm seeing a baby."

When clients adamantly argue with my predictions, fervently denying that what I am seeing or feeling is physically or logistically possible, I usually defer to their version of reality. I tell myself "Well, maybe I'm wrong" or "Maybe I'm incorrectly interpreting the energy." I then file away the vision of what I am seeing under "g" for garbage. Sometimes, though, the pictures just refuse to be deleted. It is as if someone invisible is poking me in the shoulder and insisting, "No! This is *the truth. Say it!" My vision then returns, exploding onto the screen of my mind with added intensity and more details. I have been doing readings long enough to know that these stronger predictions, in spite of their seeming impossibility and the client's denial, usually manifest in physical reality.*

"Let me go with this, Sheena," I urged her. "I could be wrong, of course, but I need to say what I'm seeing."

"'Kay." Resigned to hearing me out, Sheena shifted in her seat. This wasn't the news she wanted to hear but somehow she recognized its importance.

"It's a boy," I continued.

She groaned.

"And he's very special, probably an Indigo child. Do you know what that means?"

By this point, Sheena—not believing anything I said—was simply humoring me. She shook her head and waited patiently for more gobbledygook to come out of my mouth.

"It means your baby is one of a band of souls who are reincarnating at this time. They are highly evolved and have agreed to come back to the earth plane to help us make our transition into a higher consciousness."

"Uh-huh." Sheena's eyes were beginning to glaze over. "I think you must be seeing my dog." She sounded bored. "She's having puppies, you know."

"Sheena," I retorted, smiling, "I think I know the difference between a dog and a baby." Why, I wondered, did so many of my clients think that I could confuse a baby with their dogs, cats, or pet llamas? Either they believed they were going to have very hairy babies or they thought I was myopic!

"Hmmm," was her response, which sounded more like "Whatever!"

"And the soul of this baby has chosen you as his mother. In fact, it's your purpose to launch and protect him in this world. It's the agreement you made between your own soul and his. And somehow, your daughter . . . you have a daughter . . . yes?"

"Yes."

"She's going to follow in your wake somehow and do the same spiritual work."

"Natasha, my tubes are tied," Sheena repeated, still trying to hang on to her sanity. "You must *be seeing my dog." And she probably wanted to add,* Or are you completely nuts?

"Sheena, I know it sounds impossible. And maybe I am wrong. After all, I'm just seeing potential here. Nothing is written in stone. But I have to tell you the truth of what I see. Okay?"

"Okay." She exhaled and I heard her thinking, I'm sure this psychic in front of me is totally off her rocker.

I understand how defense mechanisms work. Reassured that I was completely batty, she could tell herself there would be no baby. What endeared Sheena to me, however, was her stoicism. A more excitable client, when told something they just didn't want to hear, would have stormed out of the room suggesting I be put in a straight jacket.

But everything I say during a reading is tape-recorded. I knew that, like so many clients before her, when my predictions actually came true, Sheena would get out the tape of her reading and ask the question, "Now what did Natasha say exactly?"

"The other thing is," I continued undeterred, "this baby will bring the two warring factions of your family together."

Sheena raised an eyebrow and I heard her thinking, How does Natasha know about my family? Uh-oh! Maybe she isn't so batty, after all. Then that could mean . . . ?

"You will get pregnant in March. But by the time you accept it, it will be too late to do anything about it . . . if you know what I mean."

Sheena eyes searched mine. She wasn't sure what to believe now.

"How will my husband react?"

Was she accepting the baby as fact now or was she just humoring me? "By the time it happens, he'll be working as a contractor making good money, feeling good. He'll be thrilled," I responded.

"How did you know he worked in construction?" she asked.

I just smiled and shrugged, not wanting to state the obvious.

"Natasha, are you sure it's not a dog?" While her tone implied amusement, she couldn't hide the hint of dread in her voice.

"It's definitely a baby." I picked up my deck of angel cards and set them down ready for her to pick three. "I would say I'm sorry, Sheena, but I know once it's all happening, you will be very happy."

"Right."

When she shuffled the deck, three cards instantly fell out onto the table. "They're the ones we use," I told her, picking them up, flipping them over, and laying them out in the correct order in front of her. "The present, your future challenge, and the outcome or advice," I explained.

Sheena stared at the cards, absorbing their implications. The smile was gone now. Present: ***New Beginnings.*** *Future Challenge:* ***Children.*** *Advice:* ***Truth and Integrity.***

"Well, if you are right, Natasha, I'll definitely be back to see you. But—and I mean this in the nicest way—I hope I never see you again."

"I totally understand," I said, grinning.

§

And now here she was, back in my chair, eight months pregnant . . . and smiling. *Phew!*

Sheena sat down, this time in the silent, cool airiness of the Solar Room, and arranged herself in a comfortable position. "Although I thought you were nuts at the time," she started, "everything you told me came true. I had to get the tape out and listen to it all over again."

How many times have I heard that?

"During the reading," she continued, "I was in so much shock, I didn't really hear anything you said—except 'baby,' of course. I did get pregnant in March, just like you said." She sat back and observed her burgeoning mound, stroking it. "I thought maybe I was just putting on weight, until May/June when I finally went to the doctor. He told me I was pregnant. The doctor and I laughed about it being a dog."

She smiled almost apologetically. I silently accepted the apology. So nice to be validated.

"Then five months into my pregnancy, John's family and my family started coming together. It was just like you said. The baby would bring about healing. And he already has."

"He?" I questioned.

"That's what I feel and that's what you said. I don't know for sure." Sheena was humble now. "But how did it happen?" she asked. "My tubes were tied."

"It's a miracle," I said. "When a soul wants to get through, nothing—no vasectomies, tied tubes, infertility, old age, or anything else—will stop it. The soul always finds a way to get in under the wire." Another client's baby, whose arrival I had predicted five years before her birth, had been conceived just a few days before her father's vasectomy. "Sometimes when the biology isn't in place—for a birth or a death—I feel the soul can make the biology change to make it fit its own agenda. This cellular change can also apply to the healing of the body in the case of terminal illnesses. Call it intention or will."

She just nodded.

"Do you have a name for your child yet?" I asked her.

With a grin on her face from ear to ear, Sheena shrugged. "My husband and I thought we might call him *Dog*."

"Or *Miracle*," I offered. We both laughed.

The following spring, Sheena made an appointment for a follow-up reading. When she showed up at my door, she was indeed clutching a beautiful blue-eyed baby boy. When I saw the light of recognition of who

I was, a light-worker, in *his* eyes, I felt validated once again. His spirit was, indeed, very, very special.

Sheena's 17-year-old daughter had accompanied her. As she dropped her mother off at my front door and took over the driver's seat, I saw in her aura that she was already carrying a light-worker's energy so she could follow in the wake of her mother and her special baby brother.

All babies, of course, are miracles, but some miracles are just more miraculous than others.

6 How Do You Explain Miracles?

Dear Natasha,

How do you explain miracles? Is it possible to create our own miracles?

Dear Miracle-Seeker,

The various dictionary definitions of the word "miracle" include:

1. An act of God: an event that appears to be contrary to the laws of nature and is attributed to some supernatural agency or regarded as an act of God.
2. An amazing event: an event or action that is amazing, extraordinary, or unexpected.
3. A marvelous example: something admired as a marvelous creation or example of a particular type of science or skill.

In the world of tick-tock mentality, as writer Stuart Wilde characterizes it, many of us still believe that miracles—where the impossible suddenly manifests—are unlikely events. We might still think that miracles have a biblical connotation, that they only appear in our lives if our god is suddenly in a good mood and feels like bestowing favors on us. Or we might think miracles occur because we were good and we are being rewarded. But while good karma definitely helps in the miracle-making department, it's not the whole story.

Miracles can be seen as both natural occurrences *and* magical events. The birth of a child, the perfect functioning of the human body, or the continuing existence of humans on this planet no matter how hard we attempt to destroy ourselves and each other could all be seen as miraculous.

As in the previous story, I often see miracles in the course of my clients' readings. These people don't believe me when I predict the impossible, not at the time of the reading anyway. The doubtful-cynical-scared attitudes evaporate, though, when those same clients call me two weeks or six months or three years later with "Ohmigod, Natasha. You were right! It's a miracle."

Yep! But maybe it wasn't a miracle. Just physics.

The universe is not chaotic. Method—in the form of the universal laws of creation—lurks within its madness.

According to quantum-consciousness thinkers, miracles are common occurrences many of us take for granted. In my own metaphysical world, they are thought forms into which I place desire, belief, and will until they become manifest. As I envision the miracle occurring, I trust that the event is for the highest good of all concerned, especially little old me. My credo is: “Anything is possible.” And the more open I am to miracles, the more they occur.

Miracles are governed by physics and psychology. Just as we can master technology for our own uses when we understand how it functions, we can also master miracles when we understand the laws of physics and psychology necessary for them to occur.

We live in an illusory world where everything we see, feel, hear, and experience is mutable and sometimes just a matter of opinion! In order to create miracles, we must first detach ourselves from the belief that everything we see is solid. Once we understand that what we *are* seeing with our human eyes is (invisible) energy that has mutated into denser mass (visible) energy, then we are making progress. For example, once upon a time someone had an idea for a table on which to place things. Idea = thought form = invisible energy. As we know, this idea *did* manifest into a table—a denser mass of energy (visible energy). To someone that table was a miracle!

Energy never dies but just changes form. This mutation of energy, therefore, can also work in reverse. Dense energy masses (visible energy) can also revert to a thought form (invisible energy). As an example, look at the true story of a man and his brain tumor as told in *My God I Thought You'd Died* by Claude Dosdall and Joanne Broatch. His tumor began as an unconscious fear-based thought form, then manifested into the physical and was seen as a detectable mass. But the person with the tumor decided that he was not ready to die and chose to heal the tumor. With intention, desire, will, and visualization as well as adjustments to diet, lifestyle, and attitude, he changed the visible back into the invisible, and the tumor disappeared. While metaphysicians understand that process as deliberate or conscious-driven, others might say it was a miracle!

Miracles can be described in these terms:

* Miracles are a rearrangement of mutable energy into a different form, instantly or gradually.
* Miracles are thought forms. These thought forms can simmer in

the ether for a long time before we are ready to receive them and before they actually appear in the physical plane.

* Miracles are a manifestation of our faith in them.
* Miracles are events that take place naturally and are merely incongruent with our current belief systems. That is, they are categorized as "unbelievable" only because they occur beyond our current level of understanding.
* Miracles are infinite potentialities. To a 17th century person, for example, sending instant messages between countries through fiber-optic cables and having them appear instantly on a computer screen would have been an impossibility—a miracle.
* Miracles are creations that we can orchestrate. We don't have to wait for the fickle finger of fate or an angelic presence to answer our prayers.

So, **dear Miracle-Seeker**, if you want to make a miracle happen, instead of begging on bended knee to some benevolent force hoping that said force is in a good mood, here's what you can do to create your own:

❖ *Intend* a miracle into existence, impossible as the result might seem. *Will* the result with absolute, undiluted faith.

❖ *Decide* that your miracle is not only possible but that it is already birthed in the ether (the invisible). With your commitment to it, turn it from thought (invisible) into matter (visible). Now all that stands between you and your miracle is space. With your magnetic thoughts, and using visualization or affirmations, bring the miracle closer and closer to you until it arrives in your world.

And remember . . .

❖ Gratitude is the foundation of abundance. Being thankful for all the miracles already manifest creates a garden in which more miracles can seed and multiply.

❖ The Universe helps those who help themselves. The Universe also grants miracles to those who are willing to believe in them and who take the necessary action to make them possible.

❖ What we focus on expands. When we focus on the magic of miracles, then what we want—instead of what we don't want—will expand in our lives.

- Choose another word for "miracle." For example, try using the term "intention," especially if your mind equates "miracle" with "impossible." Otherwise, that's exactly where your miracle will stay—out there in the realm of impossibility.

And sometimes, despite our conscious disbelief, miracles will still manifest just as Sheena's did in the previous story.

A miracle, or that which we understand as miraculous, may have been written for a long time—old karma. In Sheena's case, perhaps it was an agreement between old souls. And sometimes miracles are just heaven-sent gifts to remind us that there *are* such things as miracles and that the Universe is a magical, loving place.

HAUNTED

The invitation had sounded innocent enough. So why was my stomach doing flipflops?

"Why don't you come with us, Natasha?" Something undefined in the voice of my young psychic student and now friend, Suzanna, tugged at me.

"Where are you going exactly?" I asked, both afraid and delighted that on this beautiful spring day I would have an excuse to abandon my "to-do" list and escape the four walls of my house.

"My friend Angela's back in town. We're just going for a walk down by Salmon Creek."

The creek was just a twenty-minute scenic drive from my home through lush countryside. Somehow I knew I would be doing the driving but that wasn't what was bothering me. My intuition was partly urging me to go and partly warning me to be careful. Was it the place or the people that were suspect? There was only one way to find out.

"Well . . . ," I faltered, uncharacteristically indecisive. "Who is this Angela?" For some reason I already felt an aversion to the energy of her name.

"I've known her for about five years, but she just moved back here a little while ago," Suzanna explained.

"Well, that makes three of us," I said. Neither Suzanna nor I had lived in the area for very long.

Eight years my junior, Suzanna had come to me as a client four years earlier. Subsequently, after attending one of my psychic development courses, she had become my psychic protégée. Now we had a firm teacher/student relationship, but ever since we had met, I had not been able to shake the sense of responsibility I felt toward her. Perhaps she had been my younger sister or brother in a past life?

Probably due to the combination of her amazing psychic ability and an abusive childhood, her terrors often overwhelmed her. At such times she would call me in a panic. "Natasha! I'm becoming detached," she would cry, sounding as if she were a helium balloon about to fly into outer space never to touch earth again. I would talk her down, deflating her fears and grounding her back on the planet. She credited me with having saved her sanity more than once. I didn't argue. I know it's not easy being psychic.

"You'll like Angela," Suzanna added. "She's psychic, too."

"Uh-huh," I responded, thinking that just because someone is psychic doesn't necessarily mean I'm going to like them, though I am always happy to meet a student of metaphysics. I was surprised at my own strange, initial antipathy to Angela. I hadn't even met her and I was pushing her away.

"Do you have readings?" Suzanna knew how busy my practice was.

"Not today, actually, but . . ." *I have so much paperwork and laundry to do, I shouldn't,* I told myself. But it was a sunny March day, and after a long winter I needed sunshine on my soul. "Sure," I said finally. "Why not?"

Angela turned out to be a cherubic twenty-eight-year-old with straight, almost-black hair framing her plump cheeks. She was a combination of old-soul energy and spirited youth. Something about her seemed both familiar and a little irritating, but I couldn't put my finger on why. Maybe it was just the difference in our ages, I told myself.

Before going for our walk, we stopped for a leisurely cup of coffee at The Gallery Café, the hub of hippie-land, while Suzanna told Angela about some of her more outrageous psychic experiences. As Angela contributed her own stories, I noticed my niggling annoyance with her was turning to something stronger. Was it anger? This poor woman hadn't done anything to me. Where was this resentment coming from? Maybe it was my guilt about being here. Maybe I should have stayed at home and done my laundry after all . . . .

"So where are we going to walk?" I asked.

"Let's walk along the beach toward the creek," Angela responded, tossing her long dark hair. "I haven't been there in ages." Then suddenly she turned to me and said, "I feel I know you from somewhere, Natasha."

"Oh . . . yes?" I responded, attempting nonchalance.

"Natasha's in the paper," Suzanna stated. "Maybe you've seen her photo."

"No." Angela was peering intensely into my face. I squirmed in my seat, aware now that we both knew some kind of unpleasant truth. "No, that's not it." She shrugged and took another sip of her Americano.

I wondered, apart from our fascination with the psychic realm, if the three of us really had anything in common. Our ages and lifestyles were so disparate. The question nagged at me: why was I here? Then I rationalized that this outing probably had a higher purpose. *Just stay present and enjoy yourself,* I decided and consciously put a smile on my face.

After we finished our coffees, we ambled down the short, curved road that followed Salmon Creek to a long stretch of log-strewn and pebbled beach. "It's a good walk this way," Suzanna said, pointing to the right. As we stumbled over stones and shells, I went slightly ahead of them and allowed their animated conversation to drift away on the breeze.

Behind me, I heard Angela exclaim, "Let's go up there." I turned to see that she was pointing at a sandy, two-lane track that rose from the beach and ended in dark woodland. Then without waiting for our agreement, she skipped over the pebbly beach, scrambled over some logs, and started up the path.

After a moment's hesitation, Suzanna and I followed. When we caught up with Angela, she was standing stock still, as if listening for something.

"What's up?" I asked, thinking maybe we had inadvertently invaded somebody's back garden or that she had come face to face with a bear.

"I'm not sure . . . just a feeling." Then she shook her long mane of black hair and we carried on.

After about fifty feet the path veered into the forest, but to our left, set in a green lawn surrounded by trees and bushes, was a tiny, old, white building. Was it a church? Or had it been a school?

"What is this?" Angela asked. "Let's go look inside." She bounded up the few front stairs and pulled on the double front doors. They didn't open. "Locked." She shrugged and stood back.

For some reason I exhaled, relieved that they wouldn't let us in.

Oddly, the white doors were newly painted yet there were no notices to suggest that the building might still be used for community gatherings or as a meeting hall or a church. Instinctively I knew that this apparent innocence was somehow a lure.

"Too bad," Suzanna said. "But it's kind of cute, don't you think?"

Cute wasn't the word that sprang to my mind. "I think this place is a bit creepy," I muttered almost under my breath.

"Creepy?" Suzanna turned to face me. "Why?"

I shrugged in response. I wasn't sure yet.

But Angela had bounded back down the stairs and headed to the back of the building. As Suzanna and I followed, she commented on the deserted air of the place. "I wonder why no one uses this place?"

"Exactly!" I added, "You would think there would be all kinds of posters on the door for various activities." But there was nothing. The building didn't even have a name on it.

As Suzanna and I rounded the corner, we saw Angela jumping up in an attempt to peer inside through the darkened windows. "Nothing," she said, responding to my enquiring expression.

But as all three of us came around the next corner of the building, we saw that where a wide single door had obviously once been, a black hole gaped into the bright day. I stopped at least six feet away from the dark void, but even from there I recognized that something in that blackness was evil, its heavy energy oozing out into the sunlight. The blot reminded me of Edvard Munch's painting *The Scream*, the man on the bridge screaming, the mouth a dark oval of agonized rage.

In the shadows within the darkness I could vaguely make out a wooden staircase. As I stood transfixed, sensing that heinous events had taken place in there, the image of a tall, slim man in his early forties appeared in the doorway. He was a teacher, perhaps even the headmaster, and I knew that he was the perpetrator of the evil and that his awareness of his own sickness kept his ghost stuck in that place together with the spirit residue of his victims.

The atrocity of what he had done hit me like a sickening wave. Then, as if I had called them out of the shadows, the ghostly imprints of the boys he had sexually violated emerged, one by one. Among them were the spirits of three brothers. The terror, rage, and unresolved trauma they suffered because of the odious silence they had been forced to keep almost throbbed in that black hole. *Such a small container for such a big, vile secret*, I thought. The injustice, powerlessness, and wretchedness leached out of the blackness, contaminating the bright, sunny, blue-skied day outside.

"Let's go in," Suzanna, always the adventurous child, said.

"No . . . I think . . ." I started to say, but before I could finish, Suzanna was already swallowed up in the blackness inside the building with

Angela on her heels. I could only stand, paralyzed by fear, afraid that my two companions might be overtaken by the evil inside.

I remained rooted there in the bright sunshine, the serene stillness of this picturesque scene contrasting with the insidiousness of that black hole. The sky was blue, the grass and trees a lush green, the sun was warm, and everything was still. But why were no birds singing in this idyllic natural setting? Nor could I hear any sounds from inside the darkness, no chatter from Suzanna or Angela.

After what seemed like an eternity, they came bursting out again as if they had been spat out by some force. They blinked in the bright sunlight.

I exhaled. "What's in there?" I asked.

"Nothing much," Angela responded, but some flicker across her cherubic face told me that she was disturbed by the experience and didn't know why. Suzanna's face was ashen.

"What is it, Suzanna?"

"When I walked up the stairs that led to the kitchen," she explained almost in a whisper, "something wouldn't let me get up there. Something like a force was waiting at the top of the stairs and chased me down."

"We have to move away from here," I responded coolly, suppressing a shiver, and led them down the gentle slope toward the front of the building.

As soon as we had distanced ourselves from the doorway, Suzanna sank down on the lush grass, relieved. Angela stood facing me. "It doesn't feel good in there . . . ," she said, turning to glance back at the black hole. "Why didn't you go in, Natasha?"

Suzanna squinted up at me expectantly. "Yeah, Natasha, why didn't you?"

"You tell me." I lobbed the question back to Suzanna. "What did you feel?"

"Something evil happened in there," she said, lifting her face up to the sun, inhaling the light. "I couldn't wait to get out. It's almost suffocating."

"I'm sure . . . ," I began and faltered. Angela was still waiting for my answer. For me to put my vision into words brought up a wave of nausea. I waited for it to pass. "There's a tall, slim man, a teacher or headmaster, and he used that back stairwell to sexually abuse boys . . . orphans . . . boys no one cared about."

I heard a gasp and realized it was Suzanna. But I carried on in my psychic stream. Angela was peering hard into my eyes, an indefinable expression on her face. "I felt that later he dismembered some of them . . ." I shuddered, "with an axe . . . ."

"Ohmigod!" Suzanna's tone had a trace of recognition within it, as if she were suddenly remembering something.

"He buried them," I continued, "somewhere here, maybe in those woods." I turned and pointed to the copse on my right. Another gasp from Suzanna.

"When was this?" Angela asked eventually as if suddenly shaking herself out of a daze.

"Late last century or even up to the fifties of this century," I responded, seeing the man's clothes in my mind's eye. "I'm not exactly sure." The emotions, however, were intense. "He is so guilty that he feels he has to stay here. He's not going to leave and he wants us out of here. The vibration is so dark and low," I added, "that anyone who is too psychically open could undergo possession in there." I glanced at Suzanna, concerned that she might have succumbed, but she seemed to be her own sweet self.

"I feel three boys here," I said and felt like crying. "I can hear their screams. I can feel the outrage of the violation. Even if they had been able to tell someone, nobody would have believed them because this man appeared to be such a gentle soul and had so much respect and authority in the community. He threatened them to keep it a secret." I exhaled overwhelmed by the horror of it all. "It still is a horrible secret."

I paused to glance back at the doorway. Angela, I noticed, was still studying me intently.

"Can you help their spirits move on?" Suzanna asked, knowing that in my work I often help miserable, clingy ghosts finally leave the earth plane and return home in peace to the spirit world.

"They're not ready to. And it's too powerful and too much for me," I confessed, already feeling that the darkness in there wanted nothing to do with my light. "I have to leave this place."

I walked to the front of the white building and then continued down to the edge of the lawn. Standing in front of a hedge of overgrown bushes, I breathed in the sea air and exhaled the trauma, allowing the view of the still ocean to calm me.

Suzanna came and stood behind me while Angela lay on the grass behind us. We were all lost in silence. How could a place that appeared so charming, like a scene out of *Anne of Green Gables*, have been used for such unbearable ugliness? The duality that humans exhibit toward one another—the conflicting appetites for both brutality and human kindness—never ceases to amaze me. I allowed the line of blue on the horizon to remind me that beauty still exists in this world.

But it wasn't over yet.

Some force from behind was drawing me toward the forest. I turned away from the ocean view and walked up the lawn toward the wooded area to the left, deliberately avoiding glancing at the black hole. Just on the edge of the woods, I stopped short. The dewy, rich smell of moss filled my senses.

"What is it?" Suzanna and Angela were following me now as if I were a diviner seeking signs of water. They stood behind me, waiting.

"There's the spirit of a boy standing by that tree." I pointed to my left to an old fir on the edge of the forest. "He's shy but wants to get our attention," I said, being reminded of author Gregg Braden's statement that until we give focus to something, it doesn't exist. Seeing spirits is much like this. No wonder they feel ignored and try to make us aware of them. "And I see a clergyman standing there," I continued, turning to the right where a large tree had fallen a long time ago, its remains now covered in a ragged carpet of green lichen. "He's something like a Quaker minister or Mennonite," I said even though I knew that historically neither of those religious denominations had been reported as having lived in the area. "He's not a Protestant or a Catholic priest, anyway . . . . And when he preached, the people sat there." I turned and waved a hand at a semi-circular ring of trees, a natural amphitheatre for his pulpit.

The three of us stood staring, Suzanna and Angela trying to imagine what I could psychically see and sense.

"Is the minister a bad guy, too?" Angela asked.

"Not sure," I responded. "He taught here long before the school was built. He's not evil like the man in the school but he feels guilty as if what happened here later were his fault."

Still standing on the edge of the clearing between the woods and the school, reluctant to enter deep into the shadowy copse, all three of us envisioned our own version of this sad history.

Without speaking, we turned to leave the wooded area. Suzanna suddenly lurched forward, her hands raking the empty air for support as she fell to the ground. Angela and I went to help her up.

"Something grabbed me by the ankle!" she exclaimed, visibly shaken and brushing the earthy debris from her hands.

I peered down to see if my friend had merely tripped over tree roots, but nothing protruded from the ground. "Probably the little boy," I said, "trying to get your attention."

Suzanna suddenly shuddered and picked up her pace. "Let's get out of here."

In silent agreement, Angela and I followed. This time we walked back along the road to the café where my car was parked, the animated chatter now extinguished and replaced with deep reflection on what we had experienced. We drove home in silence through the comforting familiarity of green countryside until Angela asked almost nonchalantly from the back seat, "Natasha, what is it you're not telling us?"

My nausea instantly returned. Suzanna was right, Angela *was* psychic. Looking in my rearview mirror, I peered directly into her enquiring eyes. "The ghosts of the three boys are still stuck in there," I said, watching for her reaction. "They're brothers with big age gaps between them. The oldest brother is in more pain because he wasn't able to protect his two little brothers, especially the youngest, from this monster. He's stuck in there with not just his pain but also his guilt, rage, and anger—and not just toward the headmaster. He feels it toward the youngest brother, too. Because of him, he feels the most guilt."

"Did you get a sense of the exact ages of the boys?" she prodded, leading the conversation in a direction I knew I didn't want to go.

"Yes . . . 18, 10, and five," I responded, cognizant that the age differences were exactly the same as those between Suzanna, Angela, and me. "They were brothers . . . ," I repeated inanely. I had felt their energy and heard their cries, the trauma of their pain still reverberating, their secrecy still amplifying the trauma.

"Makes you wonder," Angela muttered, glancing out the window at the colorful shopping mall as we re-entered the town center, "why the three of us had to experience that."

Yes, I thought, despite my resistance, the whole day had had a feeling of . . . other-worldliness about it. Why *had* the three of us—an unlikely trio—been to that place? And all three of us had in some way picked up on that awful energy. "Maybe," I said, the words just coming out of nowhere and answering my own question, "*we* were the three brothers . . . ."

A low moan came from both women. What if I *had* been the older brother in that past life and had not been able to protect my two younger siblings? If Angela had been my youngest brother in that lifetime, it would explain my resistance to her now. On some level, she evoked my old feelings of guilt and helplessness. Perhaps we had come together today so we could all let the horror go and I could forgive myself? Whether this was our story, or it simply reminded us of another past life together, some soul-retrieval work would be in order to reclaim the lost pieces of our souls. If that *were* the truth, I wasn't ready for it.

A week later, Suzanna called. "Angela and I decided to do some research on that place so we went to the library, the newspaper archives, and the municipal office."

"And?"

"There was nothing official about anything horrible happening there. But it *was* used as a schoolhouse."

I groaned. Surely, if boys had been murdered in that place, something would have been recorded somewhere. But if they were orphans who no one cared about, would there be any written accounts?

"But it was what the librarian said that made our hair stand on end," Suzanna almost whispered.

"What was that?"

"Some local teenagers decided to camp in there one Friday night but ran out terrified. They said they heard the bloodcurdling screams of children."

7 Can Psychics See Their Own Futures?

Dear Natasha,

As a psychic, can you see your own future?

Dear Intuitive,

I'm happy you asked this question as people seem to judge psychics for *not* knowing everything, including their own futures.

My answer is threefold. Sometimes yes. Sometimes no. And sometimes I don't need to *predict* because I am constantly *creating* my own future. However, when I can't access my own truth, just as for everyone else it's my ego that's in the way.

Let me explain.

Before each psychic reading—and as described in my first book—I inform my clients that I am tuning in to their six levels of consciousness: the soul, the spirit, the subconscious, the unconscious, the ego, and the higher consciousness. On each consciousness level, especially the subconscious, I am able to determine what the client's beliefs are and sense what they are projecting into the future with those beliefs. It's kind of like weather forecasting: based on current conditions (subconscious beliefs), this is what will be created in the future. As happens with weather forecasters, however, my timing can be off and my interpretation of the patterns doesn't always include other minor variables.

Many of my clients' subconscious beliefs can be diametrically opposed to their ego-thinking. The discrepancy causes inner conflicts they are oblivious to. The ego believes what it wants to believe. Some clients argue with me because I often predict the opposite of what they think is true . . . in their ego-mind, at least. My readings are all taped so I just respond with "We'll see."

Because the ego is our waking state and the only level of mind that most of us are fully cognizant of—while awake anyway—it is understandable that we think our ego is our only reality. But the ego, compared to the other levels, is like a pea-brain, God bless it. The ego is also the only part of our minds that experiences the concepts of fear and separation. This pea-brain will, therefore—out of fear—become attached to ideas, places, and people. And the ego doesn't like to be wrong. Caught up in identity, the illusion-filled ego is more about how things seem and how people appear on the surface. The other levels of consciousness, meanwhile, give us the wider scope of non-attachment and truth. While the poor old ego is often portrayed as "bad," something to be squelched or disposed of, we *do* all need an ego. Instead of castigating it, we can embrace our pea-brain and be grateful that we have an ego since, despite its limitations, its functions are necessary for our sanity.

One of the ego's valuable jobs is to filter the information with which we are bombarded on a daily basis. Our minds would otherwise be overwhelmed with information, and we would be far more insane than we already are. Okay. Maybe I should just speak for myself here!

Another function of the ego is to make us aware of fear so we can learn discernment between love-based and fear-based emotions. On this spiritual path we're on, in order to ascend to the lighter vibrations, we must first become conscious of the darker forces. The ego is the filter for all those energies, light and dark.

When I am reading my clients, my gift lies in being able to bypass their egos and see what is held in all the other five levels of consciousness, like looking under a beautiful (pea-green) Persian rug. The carpet (ego) may exhibit a beautiful pattern but when I peer underneath the carpet (into the subconscious), I can see what is hidden—the other beliefs that actually determine what we do and don't attract. Based on those beliefs, I am able to prognosticate for my clients how those deeper patterns of thinking will determine their future outcomes.

Unfortunately, I can't always see under my own carpet (into my subconscious) because my own ego is in the way, also trying to convince me that I am right about what I want to believe. My deeper truth might be more uncomfortable, even painful. I may opt to ignore the truth and that's when I, the psychic, just like others, can get into trouble.

Another analogy is being in the eye of the hurricane. As a psychic to others, I can see through the turbulence that surrounds them and I can see the center eye where all is clear. But being at the center of my own hurricane, I cannot see my own eye. The turbulence around me is all that's in my periphery. Just as psychologists are required to get counseling from their peers for mental health, I also voluntarily check in with my own psychic friends at those times.

Because I understand how the ego works, of course, I focus more on my intuition. I have lived my life being sensitive to my inner voice. My intuitive warnings have saved my life more often than I care to admit. My angels have, no doubt, been very busy protecting me. When I choose to ignore the wisdom of that intuitive guidance, like the rest of humanity

I have to pay the consequences until I get back on track. And I berate myself for not having followed the guidance.

When I am experiencing heavier emotions like grief, fear, or anger, tuning in to myself becomes tricky, because like everyone else I am invested in my emotions and I am attached to a certain outcome. In order to see the truth, however, I must remain neutral, detached. The truth is—and seeing the truth is what being psychic means—one must completely let go of the narrow lens of one answer, of being right or wrong. Being detached enables me to widen the lens and see the whole picture.

At other times, negative events that manifest in my life come without warning. I recognize these dramas as karmic lessons that I am meant to experience as part of my own soul journey. If I *could* foresee those events, I might avoid them and never learn the lesson. Then, I believe, I would have to reincarnate and do them all over again. No thanks!

Malaise, fear, or celebratory joy are general feelings from which I can sometimes predict my future, but the movie-like details that accompany those feelings and that I am normally able to see for my clients can sometimes completely elude me. For example, three days before Princess Diana's death, I felt a huge dread that seemed to portend an imminent disaster of global proportions, but when I asked my mind for details, none came to me. I surmised that an asteroid would hit the planet that weekend. And metaphorically it did. Some things we are just not meant to see.

As a psychic and metaphysician for 30-plus years, I have metaphysical tools at my disposal, of course. I habitually tap into my own intuitive "kit bag" such as dream interpretation, meditation, visualization, affirmations, astrological readings, numerological influences, and pendulum divining. But my psychic colleagues are often the ones who validate my feelings, give me a more detailed and enlightened perspective on what is transpiring, and confirm what I already know but don't necessarily trust. I do the same for them. Seeing through others' egos is so much easier than bypassing one's own pea-brain!

For me, the quest to understand the universal laws of energy is constant. The patterns of my own life are also my laboratory but still, and this may shock you, I don't know everything. Not yet, anyway.

What I do know is that intuition and sensory energy technology will become more and more important parts of how we function. Chaos often precedes rapid growth. As the frequencies on the planet continue to increase in vibration and the pace of our lives accelerates, the benefit of a honed intuition to guide us through the turbulence of these changes may no longer be a luxury but instead just might save our bacon. What might have previously made sense will no longer fit in the new world. The only guidance that can be relied upon might be the voice right inside us, the voice of intuition.

So, **dear Intuitive,** psychics are just human beings with an added layer of sensitivity that allows them to tune in to other people and other dimensions. We all have that capability, if we develop it. And we all have an ego. Whether we use our sensory perception to predict what will unfold or we determine to create our own future is our choice. We all have the power to do both, and maybe that's all we need to know—for now anyway.

8

IN THE PSYCHIC NET

"What are the nightmares about?" I asked my friend, Becky. Because I am an avid dream interpreter, other people's nighttime reveries always fascinate me, but in this case, the nightmares were those of Becky's daughter, eight-year-old Sophia, a little girl who had already demonstrated extraordinary psychic abilities. I felt especially protective toward her.

"She says this magician invites her to come and play. And he taunts her."

"Poor Sophia," I shuddered. "It sounds creepy." I was well aware that low-life spirits often mess with children's energy, especially while they are asleep and vulnerable. Sophia was particularly empathetic to energy. "How long has this been going on?"

"Oh, for months now. She's been waking me up in the middle of the night screaming," Becky answered wearily, obviously pining for undisturbed sleep. "She troops up to my room, half-asleep, and climbs into my bed."

I had my reasons for being particularly interested in Sophia's nocturnal experiences. When Rachel, her older sister, had still been a baby, I had predicted that within five years Becky would have another child, a very special girl. Despite her protestations of "no way" and "over my dead body," I told her that it was in her soul contract and that, whatever Becky did or did not do, this child would be born anyway. Maybe it was little comfort to Becky at the time, but I also added that the child would be a highly evolved soul, very psychic, and that she had in another lifetime been Becky's grandmother. Her role would be as teacher to her mother as her mother would be to her.

Five years after my prediction, Becky's husband had smugly announced,

"See, I told you we wouldn't have any more children." But the smile disappeared from his face the very next day when Becky reported she was pregnant. Thus, Sophia had come to the world on cue and very soon exhibited signs of being an unusually aware child.

Now, in the spring of 2002—eight years after Sophia's birth—on my regular bi-monthly visit to the oceanside resort town of White Rock to do psychic readings, I was staying overnight at Becky's house. Usually on these two-day events, I crashed on Becky's living room couch. On this particular night both Sophia and Rachel were staying overnight at their father's house—Becky and her husband were divorced by this time—so I slept in the girls' bedroom.

After performing six readings that day, I retired early feeling weary. Above Sophia's bed, off-white netting draped down from a circular wooden ring. The material surrounded her pillows, which were laden with furry animals and toys. At night as she slept, the netting would be pulled around her, enclosing her head and shoulders to create an illusion of protection. But now I felt the netting was having the opposite effect. In fact, I shuddered every time I looked at it, so, like Goldilocks, I gratefully snuggled under the covers of Rachel's bed instead. And in that place between consciousness and sleep, I became aware that I wasn't alone in the room.

With my face turned toward the velvet-curtained windows, I felt the spirit of an older man hovering in front of and just above me. Then I realized at least one more spirit, a darker entity, was standing at the foot of Sophia's bed. I recognized him as "the magician." His thick, dark energy was menacing, and I sensed the smirk on his face. He was looking for Sophia but she wasn't there. I was.

At first my whole body tensed in fear against these thick presences. But then quickly I reminded myself that I was a psychic, for god's sake. I knew what to do. After all, they were just spirits, like people but without physical bodies. I could talk to them just as I talk to the living.

I dealt first with the one over my bed, the least offensive.

What are you doing here? I asked telepathically.

I just like being here came the reply.

Don't you want to go home to the light? I urged.

No, I'm happy here.

I sensed that he posed no danger to the girls. His energy felt harmless. If he wanted to stay, that was up to him, I thought. He was merely an observer, wanting to enjoy their childish innocence.

Now for the next spirit. The dark, murky spirit of the magician over by Sophia's bed was so ominous I didn't even want to engage him in dialogue. When I asked my guides what his purpose for being there was, the response came: "to toy with Sophia's energy." Maybe this entity was into magic, but not the light-hearted innocent kind. He definitely didn't make me feel warm and fuzzy.

Did the magician have something to do with the netting around Sophia's bed? Although the material was physically clean, there was something grubby, even dirty, about the way it hung there. Perhaps something was caught in its fibrous web? The magician? I wondered if this dark spirit had first been attracted to Sophia as a light-filled psychic playmate with her innocent clean spirit. But then perhaps his energy residue had become entangled in the netting's thin nylon fibers like a spider in its web, and that's why he had stayed.

In my mind I firmly told him to go away, to leave little Sophia alone. Although somehow I knew this lower vibrational spirit would never entertain the thought of listening to me and leaving the physical plane, I still urged him to go home to the light. But he was having too much fun taunting Sophia who, being psychically so wide open, was especially vulnerable. I was determined—he had to go.

So I envisioned Sophia's bed in a white bubble of light, the netting gone, and this nasty spirit—and any others who might be lurking in the corners of the room—no longer able to disturb her sleep. As I finally succumbed to sleep myself, I made a mental note to tell Becky to sage the girls' room.

When I walked into the kitchen the next morning to put on coffee, the house was unusually quiet, almost hushed. Becky wasn't up yet—for which I was grateful. She is a don't-talk-to-me-before-I've-had-two-cups-of-coffee person, so I reminded myself that unless I wanted my head bitten off, I would need to have a cup of coffee in her hand before I told her of last night's events. And I would definitely have to tell her—whether she liked it or not—because I had to go home and she would have to deal with the spirit in Sophia's room alone. When Becky appeared in the kitchen doorway, her brown eyes were unusually wide and alert.

"I have something to tell you," we said in unison. Then we both gasped and laughed, breathless.

"You first," I offered, pouring coffee into her favorite mug.

"I had this horrible dream . . . ," she began, her eyes scared and huge now, her long, black, tousled hair splaying over her shoulders, appearing every bit the psychic that she was still in denial of being. "I dreamt," she said, taking the coffee mug and adding cream, "that I was sleeping in this huge spooky old house with lots of empty rooms. You were the only other person there."

Uh-oh. I thought I knew what was coming.

"And when you came down the next morning, you told me the house was full of ghosts . . . "

Oh, dear. The still percolating coffee was making rude gurgling noises as if the magician's spirit were laughing at both of us.

" . . . and then you left me alone, and that night I had to sleep there all by myself in this big haunted house." She stared at me for a moment. "It's true, isn't it? You're heading home today . . . ." No need for more words. Through eye contact we just acknowledged the inevitable. It was Friday and her children wouldn't return until Sunday evening. Becky would, indeed, have to sleep there all by herself—alone except for the ghosts in the girls' room.

I poured my own coffee and together we went into the living room. Becky curled herself into the Queen Anne chair, and the leather squeaked as I plunked myself down on the couch.

"What did you want to tell me?" She caressed her coffee mug, comforted by the warmth it gave her.

"Well . . . "

"What?" she asked anxiously, seeing my pained expression. Though Becky has a hard time owning up to it, she is probably more psychic than yours truly.

I recounted my experiences of the previous night and then added, "And you need to get rid of that netting. Somehow it's attracting the spirits."

"I had a feeling about that . . . ."

Of course she did. "And clean out all the clutter," I urged, convinced that the joker of the previous night wasn't the only "low life" who was bothering Sophia. Often spirits attach themselves to things. Some of those hand-me-down toys might have brought with them more than just scratches and dents. "And sage the room. *Really* sage it."

Becky nodded, staring intently into her cup. "You think that's why she's been having nightmares, don't you?"

"Probably. She's so psychic, and that magician spirit gave me the creeps."

Becky's eyes widened. "And I have to sleep here by myself tonight . . . "

"Yes," I muttered, feeling bad at having to abandon my friend to a haunted house. "I do have to get home today . . . my dog . . . ."

Becky sat up in her chair. "It's just like the dream!" She took a huge gulp of coffee.

"Yes, it is. I'm sorry."

"It's okay." She gave me a half-smile, but I knew she didn't really feel safe staying alone in her haunted house.

A week later I called Becky to find out how she was surviving.

She laughed, "Oh, you would be proud of me." Becky always resorted to the ridiculous in "bad" situations. I breathed a sigh of relief, my own guilt about abandoning her melting. "Remember Renee?" Becky was saying.

Renee was Becky's next-door neighbor and a psychic wannabe.

"Yes . . . ?"

"Well, I convinced her to come over here and help me. First, we took down the netting and burned it in the back garden. Then we trooped through every room, like Celtic priestesses of old, candles and smoldering sage in hand, chanting incantations, praying, and ordering all the low-life unwelcome spirits to vacate." Becky was giggling now. Good sign. "Renee kept saying to the spirits, 'You're dead. So just get over it. Now leave!'"

"Do you think it worked?" Sometimes getting rid of pesky spirits can take a few sessions.

"Well, for this whole week Sophia's slept peacefully all through the night."

I exhaled.

"Thank you," Becky added with intense gratitude.

Sometimes it takes a whole village . . . of psychics . . . to raise a child.

8 What Are My Nightmares Telling Me?

Dear Natasha,

For ten years, the same violent nightmare has been waking me up. What can I do?

Dear Restless,

Believe it or not, most nightmares want to help you. The good news is that once you understand the root of your nightmare and take whatever action is needed, the nightmare will cease.

Nightmares can be categorized into three main types. Reasons for them vary and sometimes overlap:

❖ ***Single nightmares***, bad dreams that occur only once, can be caused by:
  * your subconscious warning you to do or not do something
  * your subconscious fears, whether real or not, about your current or a future situation
  * negative reactions to food (I'm serious!).

  Whatever the cause of your nightmare, you would be wise to pay attention to the literal or symbolic interpretation of the dream and take preventive action. You can follow the numbered steps below to assist you in interpreting the dream.

❖ ***Recurring nightmares*** are caused by your subconscious trying persistently to get your attention. The nightmares are like messengers surfacing from the depths of your subconscious and knocking on the door of your conscious mind to wake you up ('scuse the pun) to a deeper truth. For example, when we are hurt, we get angry and then feel guilty for the angry thoughts. We then expect to be punished for those angry thoughts and fear the punishment we think we deserve. Your violent dreams, then, likely mean that repressed and unexpressed hurt/anger/guilt feelings are lying unprocessed in your subconscious mind. Excavating the root emotion and reconciling the emotions around the event will set you free, and the nightmare will cease. Forgiveness of self and others is often the answer. However, you may need assistance in interpreting the symbolism of the dream to help you access those deep emotions.

❖ ***Psychic nightmares*** are caused by psychic attacks by low-life spirits that materialize in our dream state to scare us. Psychic attacks can involve "spinning," the feeling that you are being lifted into the air and spun around and around, unable to put your feet back on the ground. As in the previous story, children, especially more psychically sensitive children, are often vulnerable to low-life spirits who just love to mess with their energy while they sleep. Adults can also be susceptible to these opportunistic entities. Usually the low-life spirits attach to people who are:

* psychically opening up but still untrained and therefore vulnerable
* choosing fear over love
* experiencing a hole in their aura caused by:
  - a lack of groundedness after giving power away to someone or something
  - violated boundaries as the result of abuse
  - co-dependency that has left them with no boundaries
  - addictive behaviors and substances used to numb pain
  - depression that covers a suppressed anger or a chemical imbalance.

The psychically vulnerable can visualize themselves and their beds enveloped in a bubble, pyramid, or tent of white light before they go to sleep at night. Surrounding oneself or a child with light is a good protective measure against nighttime psychic attacks. And just to make sure, also invite the angels to come and watch over you or the child while you sleep.

So, dear Restless, though most of us rarely give credence to our dreams, the longer we ignore these messages, the more intense the messages will become. The repetitive theme in your recurring nightmare can provide you with the learning that will set you free.

The following process will help you bring your dream to your waking state, consciously identify the message of the dream, and then take the necessary action. Once you are back in your power, the dream will no longer have any power over you.

1. Identify at what age the dream began.
2. Search your mind for the event or the fear that might have triggered the angst.

3. Write out the whole dream as you first experienced it. List your feelings throughout the dream.
4. Divide the dream into two parts:
   a. the situation, for example, *I am walking down the road.*
   b. what happens in the situation, for example, *a bear starts chasing me.*
5. Role play each character or object in your dream. For example, if you are the bear doing the chasing, what is your motivation? What message is each character (object, event) communicating to you—powerlessness, guilt, anger, hurt?
6. Ask yourself what you are really afraid of in the dream? How does it relate to something in your past or present life?
7. Imagine how you would re-write the ending in this dreamed sequence of events so that you overcome your fear and emerge the victor.
8. Rewrite the dream. Repeat the original beginning, but rewrite the ending the way you want the story to end. For example, *I turn to face the bear and realize it is my best friend dressed in a costume having fun.*

Now, having stepped into your power, you are the victor. Your dream antagonist's aggression—which represents your fear in the dream—has evaporated, and you can experience peace.

Continue to let your dreams be your guides.

Sweet dreams!

9

THE PSYCHIC AND THE CONS

"Dave is your next reading." Helen, the ever-efficient manager of the bookstore where I did my psychic sessions two days a week, inclined her head toward him.

The tall, slim man standing in a shadowy corner wasn't one of the usual visitors to this urban metaphysical oasis. As my Scottish girlfriend would have said, "He looked a wee bit rrrufff around the edges."

"Dave?" I addressed the back of his plaid shirt. He turned and eyed me, giving me a not-so-subtle up-and-down inspection. "Hi, I'm Natasha," I said.

When we shook hands, I was not surprised by the calloused roughness of his palms. Although he was cleanly dressed in a cotton shirt and new, freshly pressed blue jeans, his unshaven chin and yellowed teeth gave him a just-off-the-street-and-gone-clean appearance. But it was his suspicious glare that gave him away. I had worked with street kids, and many of them had scrutinized me in that same I-don't-trust-anybody-so-don't-mess-with-me glare.

"Come in." I turned and ushered him toward the reading room at the rear of the store.

Even before he sat down on the other side of the table, he said, "I used to see that other psychic . . . the blonde one . . . what's-her-name?" He waved a nicotine-stained hand in the air. "But she really pissed me off," he snarled as he sat down.

That should have been my first clue.

His short fingers and chewed-on nails were additional signs of potential anger issues. *Uh-oh,* I thought, *it wouldn't take much to enrage this man.* And which psychic was he referring to? Five or six counselors worked out of this bookstore at any given time. Of course, I should have asked what the poor psychic had done to offend him, but part of me didn't want to know. Instead, after pressing the "record" and "play" buttons on my tape deck, I instructed Dave to give me his hands, palms upwards.

As I tuned in, I gave him my regular preamble—that the soul is on a journey through time and that I am merely reading a projection of his own energy. "My timing," I warned him, "can be really off sometimes. When things happen, it is also up to the—"

"I don't care about that stuff," he snapped.

Oh, joy. This man was going to be a difficult read. *How long was his session booked for? Thirty minutes . . . of hell.*

"So what is it you need?" I asked, dreading the response.

"I've got these questions." He pulled a grubby piece of folded white paper from his jeans pocket.

"I can answer questions," I replied confidently. Maybe this reading wouldn't be that bad after all.

"You see, this friend of mine—his name's George—me and him are designing a new engine for cars. I designed it. It saves a lot of energy. Do you think George is going to screw me over?"

Oh, brother. "This isn't the normal way I do readings," I said gently. "I prefer to tune into the flow and then answer questions at the end." *Especially when the questions are all negative,* I thought but didn't say out loud.

"I just need to know this stuff." He sat back from the table and slung one long, skinny, stiff-denim-clad leg over the other.

"Okay." I was dubious. "I'll see what I can do." I closed my eyes, and, taking Dave's hands again, tuned in to George. "Is he a much older guy?"

"Yeah." He frowned. "In his 60s, I think. Why? Is he going to die?"

"Oh . . ." It was my turn to frown. "No." I tried to stay focused on the first question. "He really wants to help you."

Dave grunted. "He doesn't think I'm crazy?"

"That's not what I'm getting. You can trust this man. Listen to what he has to say to you because I feel he knows what he's talking about."

"Yeah." Dave sniffed. "He's an ex-teacher of engineering at Calgary University."

"Wow. That's great."

"Why?" he asked, suspicious again.

I opened my eyes and peered straight into his. "It's great that you've attracted someone of such high caliber who can help you. That's not always easy . . . for anyone."

"Do you think there should be a 1/16-inch or 1/18-inch gap in the carburetor? See, I think it should be 1/18 inch because it would save a hell of a lot on gas consumption, and that's the whole idea."

Lordie, Lordie. This was going to be a lo-o-o-ng half hour. Dave's constant barrage of questions wasn't allowing me to stay in my psychic flow. Queries normally come at the end of the reading, and his interrogation style kept pulling me out of that place where I get my information. Each time he asked me something, I had to refocus, but he wouldn't let me go with the flow of that thought before he pounced on me with a completely different line of thinking. It was exhausting.

When the tape finally clicked, a signal that his thirty minutes were up, I exhaled. While this man was quite possibly a genius—or crazy—I still admired his determination to clean up his alcoholism, get off the streets, and begin a new life because so many people can't or won't. However, his old fear of failure and his mistrust of others would probably sabotage his otherwise creative efforts.

"The message for you, Dave, is to trust more and be open to the fact that these people are on your side. They *do* want to help you with your idea."

As Dave was leaving, buoyed by the positive reading, I reminded him, "Remember what I said about the timing. It can be way off-base, so be patient and trust."

"Thank you," he said and gave my hand another rough but slightly warmer squeeze before he left the room.

In the bookstore the following day, I was delighted to see Renate, a regular client who had become a friend. A realtor and first-generation Canadian from Germany, Renate had been particularly impressed with my last reading. At the time, she had just found a property for her son and his family in a suburb of Langley but had not yet made an offer. When I saw a telepathic view of the house in the reading, I got a really cold feeling and told her that her daughter-in-law would refuse to live there.

"Vell, vere vill zey liff?" she inquired in her soft accent.

A whole new scene unfolded in my mind, which I described to her. "Their house is close to you in White Rock."

"Oh, no, zey can't afford it zere. It is too expensiff."

"It's a steal of a deal," I assured her. "The house looks dilapidated on the outside but it's gorgeous on the inside. And it's a two-storey so they can rent out the bottom for additional income. And," I added, "your daughter-in-law will love it, especially the garden that needs some work."

The light in Renate's eyes dulled in disbelief. "I don't vant to argue wiz you, Natasha, because I know you are so good, but I tsink zat's impossible. I know all ze properties for sale in my area."

I wasn't going to give in to her limited view of the future. I saw what I saw and I knew what I knew. "It's not on the market yet," I explained. "The house will go on sale on Saturday." Then I added, somewhat surprised by my own specifics, "The deal will be sealed on the following Tuesday."

Arguing with a client about a future they cannot yet envision is a complete waste of energy. Metaphorically speaking, I can see over the top of the hill to what's on the other side while the client's thinking is sometimes so limited he or she isn't even willing to look *up* that metaphysical hill. The client can't see or often doesn't even want to entertain a different and better outcome.

A week later Renate sent me a note. It stated she was "totally in awe of the accuracy of your reading." She described how she had been driving down the street on the Saturday and felt guided to turn left. Then she saw a realtor just sticking a "For Sale" sign in the front lawn of a house. Renate pulled over immediately. When she entered the property, she knew it would be perfect for her son and his wife. The house, as I had described, needed an exterior paint job but it was beautiful on the inside, and the suite downstairs was rentable. The garden needed some work, but her daughter-in-law would be thrilled to get her hands dirty in it.

It hadn't taken Renate long to realize that this house was the one I had envisioned. Her confirmation was the low price. She instantly made an offer on behalf of her family. When the young couple saw the property, they fell in love with it and the deal was indeed sealed the following Tuesday.

Since then, Renate had referred several friends to me for readings. And now she was standing in the bookstore, introducing me—her "amazink" psychic—to her Swiss friend Ingrid.

"You vill haff a lot in common," Renate affirmed as she presented Ingrid. "She iss also a flight attendant."

"Great," I responded as I smiled and shook Ingrid's hand. Having flown for eight years, I know that flight attendants are generally fun, open-minded people—the ones I had worked with were, anyway.

"I'll come back," Renate told Ingrid. "I know you vill haff a vonderful experience."

Ingrid was, I guessed, in her mid-fifties. Initially I was not deterred by her slightly Teutonic body language. I once spent a year in Switzerland so I know that even the Swiss are cognizant of their own stiffness.

Once we were seated and comfortable, I began my preamble.

"Ja, ja," she snapped. "I just vant to know some sings about my family in Svitzerland."

Oh, no, not another one, I thought, still tired from Dave's session the previous day. "What is it you would like to know?" I asked oh so patiently.

"I am going to Svitzerland zis week. My father is extremely ill, und ja, he is going to die soon. Ve know zat. But zere are some questions about ze vill."

Again I tuned in and gave Ingrid a description of scenes as I saw them unfolding, how the estate would be distributed, how the dynamics of her family would change, and how she would have a peace-making session with her estranged brother. But to every single prediction, she only huffed and puffed, "No, no! Zat is impossible," or "Zat vould never happen."

As Monty Python would say, I didn't come here for an argument. Not even for five minutes, let alone an hour. I was tempted to say, "Let's just forget this and you can leave now." But my pride was in the way. *I am a good psychic,* I reminded myself. *And I will be letting Renate down if I allow this woman to disempower me.* No, I had to see it through. Yet finishing sixty minutes with Ingrid would be akin to a week in a dentist's chair. When I told her she would be going to Thailand soon, she positively guffawed. "I have just come back from Thailand! Vhy vould I go zere again?"

"I don't know exactly," I said, sighing, "but I see it as a holiday, not work. And you're going with a female, a good friend. It's as if she has won the trip or some money and doesn't want to go alone so she invites you. She pays for the whole thing." I smiled, trying to infuse a little lightness into the session, a levity I wasn't feeling. "Lucky you!"

Her response was merely another "Hrrumph."

"Are you in a relationship now?" I asked.

"No." Her shoulders tightened.

"Well, I have some good news. You're going to meet a man who actually feels as if he's your soul mate. You will meet him either before or after you go to Thailand but very soon. He is also European, and you're going to be very happy."

This brought a partial, subtle softening to her face quickly followed by a mild you-are-full-of-it sneer. I couldn't help wondering, if she knew everything, why she had bothered to visit a psychic.

Finally, as we neared the end of the reading, I reiterated that I always tell the truth of what I see. "I can be wrong, of course, but I also have a high accuracy rate. Keep an open mind," I added, knowing that even as I spoke, my words were evaporating unheard into thin air.

I was just about to put a new tape in my cassette deck in preparation for my next client when someone knocked hesitantly at the door. Helen stepped in. Her obvious discomfort told me she was about to impart bad news.

"Oh, Natasha!"

"What's the matter?" I asked, thinking perhaps someone had died.

"That lady, she's unhappy with her reading."

"Who? Ingrid?"

"Yes. She's saying in a loud voice in front of the other customers that you don't know what you're talking about, that you're a con." Apart from being insulted, I didn't find her behavior surprising. The woman had been so rude.

"Well, give her the money back," I told Helen without hesitating.

"Are you sure?" Helen, I could tell, felt somehow responsible.

"Absolutely," I stated, already counting out the bills. "I don't need her negativity in my aura," I added, shuddering at the thought.

Understanding, Helen nodded. "Do you want to do it?" she asked, obviously not relishing the thought of dealing with the Dragon Lady herself.

"Sure," I responded, opening the door. "I'd be happy to."

As I stepped out into the store, five other customers had their heads buried in books, others were caressing the various gems and jewelry on the shop's wooden shelves. Renate, who was standing next to the tight-lipped Ingrid, was twitching in her own skin with embarrassment.

"I understand, Ingrid, that you weren't happy with the reading," I said in a low voice.

She barely nodded, not having the courtesy to look me in the eyes.

"Well, here's your money." I had folded the bills into a slim finger-like roll which I slipped surreptitiously into her purse.

"Tsank you," she said quietly, and for the first time I saw a small smile creep up around her lips. It occurred to me it was a smile of triumph. Renate gave me a cursory I'm-so-sorry glance as both women left the store.

"I'm not surprised," I told Helen after they had left. "She acted as of she didn't believe anything I said. But we'll see. We'll see."

As it turned out, Dave was so happy with his reading that he returned the next week and the next. Thus, I was a little stunned with what happened four weeks later.

It was a Friday and I had been busy at home all day, catching up with my domestic duties, the physical work always a welcome respite from the intensity of psychic readings. As a result, I didn't get around to checking my e-mails until the end of the day. But when I finally sat down at the computer, I noticed three e-mails in my inbox from Dave.

The first one, sent at 9:42 a.m., stated that he was "pissed off" at me because nothing I had said had come true. The second one, sent at 11:51 a.m., stated that he thought "all psychics were full of s..." and he wanted his money back for all three readings, a total of $180.00. The third e-mail, sent a mere 70 minutes after the second, stated that I was a con and that if he didn't hear from me immediately he would report me to the RCMP for fraud.

Lovely! So Dave really *does* have anger issues, especially with psychics, I thought.

My reply:

Dear Dave,

Just so you know. I have a no-questions-asked, full-refund policy for all my clients if they are not happy with their sessions. As I stated at the time, there are no guarantees in psychic readings. However, if you are not happy with your session, all you have to do is ask *for a refund. I do not appreciate being threatened.*

For your information, I have been a psychic for thirty years with a very good reputation for accuracy and high integrity and you are the only person I have had to refund, except, strangely enough, for one woman a few weeks ago. Perhaps you are related?

I will make sure that your money is ready for you to pick up at the bookstore by next Tuesday. Do not threaten or contact me again. Good luck with your project. I know that during my readings I speak my truth. Have a nice life.

The following week, Dave responded by e-mail:

I got the money. Thank you. A lot of the things you told me have now come true. I think you are the best psychic in town. When can I get my next reading?

Er . . . I don't think so.

Dear Dave,

Find yourself another psychic.

Two days later, Renate called. We hadn't spoken since the "Ingrid incident." After some chit-chat about her affairs, she asked me, "Do you remember my friend Ingrid?"

You mean the client from hell number two? "Yes," I said.

"Vell, I have to tell you zis. Ingrid *did* go to Thailand, just like you said. Her girlfriend had two tickets and her boyfriend let her down so Ingrid vent for free."

Is there any justice in this world? I wondered.

"And she did meet zis guy who she is so happy with."

No. Definitely no justice!

"She also told me that ze family vill is being administered fairly and zo she has made peace with ze brother as you predicted. And . . . ," I couldn't bear to hear additional good tidings for the grumpy Ingrid—even if I had predicted them myself. But Renate continued, "I asked her if she is going to pay you ze money now."

"Oh. You can tell her I would happily receive it. But what did she say?"

"She said she would pay you ze next time she comes for a reading."

Not! "Sorry, Renate, but I won't be reading Ingrid again."

"Vhy not?"

Apart from Ingrid and Dave having qualified for my psychic blacklist, where do I start? I thought. *But their conniving karma is their problem, not mine.*

"I only choose to deal with people—clients or otherwise—who operate from integrity, not manipulation," I told Renate. "Too many people in this world genuinely respect and need my gift for me to waste it on people who . . . er . . . don't."

Needless to say, I never did hear from Ingrid again. I am psychic enough to know that she never had any intention of getting another reading or of paying me for the first session.

What was the lesson for me in my movie with these two characters? As I am constantly reminding my clients, listen to your intuition. If I had listened—and acted upon my instinct at the onset of each reading, I would have refused to read either person. Since then I reserve the right—if the vibration with the client doesn't feel right—to just say No!

But the greatest revenge is to live well . . . and to become a writer!

9 Why Can't Psychics Read Me?

Dear Natasha,

I have been to see several psychics who tell me they can't read me. Why is that?

Dear Unreadable,

While I have never been unable to read a client, I have learned that people open up their minds to different degrees. Simply put, some people are easier to read than others. I can't speak for the psychics who found you unreadable but I am sure you thought:

- that you must have reminded them of their wicked step-mother
  or
- that they must have seen something awful in your future and they didn't want to be the messenger.

If the latter were the case, at least these psychics had the good grace—and the good sense—to keep their mouths shut and their damaging visions to themselves—unlike the English clairvoyant in chapter one of *Aaagh! I Think I'm Psychic.* This supposedly seasoned psychic committed the ultimate crime of leaving her young, highly vulnerable client in a vat of hopelessness with fatal results. All of us, psychics and clients, have to remember psychics can and often do misinterpret the energy.

Psychics can't read you—or don't want to read you—for several reasons. Far from impending disasters or personality conflicts interfering with the reading, it is often the client who energetically blocks the seer and makes it difficult or even downright impossible for the information to come through. The most likely reason that you are unreadable is that you are blocking the reader with your own energy.

Let me explain.

When I hear my clients comment that some other psychic "wasn't very good" or that "I don't know who she was talking about but it sure wasn't me," my question to them is, "And how good were *you* at being open?"

As in any relationship, you have to give in order to get. A psychic reading is also an exchange. You, as the client, open up the door to your soul and let the psychic in so he or she can read you. But don't worry—you're still in charge of how much information you make available.

Opening up to a psychic—or any stranger for that matter—requires trust. I am frequently amazed—and honored—at how my new clients are willing to instantly lay their souls bare. However, I also sense when clients put up their psychic wall and won't allow me to see the whole picture. Consciously or unconsciously, they are refusing to let me in.

We all have reasons to protect our inner selves. The following are, in my experience, the most common:

1. The client already knows a truth, consciously or subconsciously, that he is not yet willing to hear.
2. The client is afraid that the psychic will see terrible things in her future.
3. The client believes he has something to hide, or feels guilty, and is not ready to be totally seen.
4. The client doesn't really believe in the process—the psychic's ability to see. Doing a reading is a test of their talent. When the client is completely blocked, the psychic is usually unable to see anything but a white fog. The seer then informs the client, "I'm sorry. I can't read you." Et voilà! Because the Universe will always make us right about what we believe, the client feels validated. "Ah-ha. I knew it! I *am right.* This is all a bunch of hocus pocus," the smug, cynical client might say as she storms off into the sunset holding ever so tightly onto a set of precious, limited, and limiting beliefs.

Having personally experienced the magic of limitless thinking, I can only feel compassion for the psychically cynical. To live in an it-only-exists-if-I-can-see-it world would be for me so monotonous. But I also know that the levels of understanding of people in that world are in another stage of evolution. And that's okay. I am not here to make anyone right or wrong, just to speak my truth, but at the same time, I refuse to waste my energy proving something that I already know to be true for me.

Perhaps if you have a deeper understanding of how psychics function, generally speaking, it may help you to choose the right psychic and to experience more trust in the sitting. Perhaps then the psychic *can* read you. The following information might be helpful:

❖ Being discerning when selecting a psychic is critical. While most psychics are caring, spiritual healers, others can be drama queens or just plain mean. Some psychics *are* psycho—an occupational hazard apparently! And even the best of us—with the highest intentions to heal and enlighten—can still misinterpret your energy.

- Psychics are paid to *know the unknowable*. Such a responsibility can create a certain pressure to deliver a morsel of infinite wisdom. Hence, psychics sometimes rush to overlay their own limited perceptions on what they see. This impulse may lead to inaccurate readings.
- Psychics might tell you bad news. However, the good news is that even after receiving negative predictions, you *can* change your thinking and subsequently completely eradicate—or drastically minimize—your negatively predicted outcomes.
- Psychics' accuracy rates vary greatly, so seek out a psychic who empowers you to trust your own intuition. If her words support you on your journey, great! If what the psychic says does not resonate with you, *let it go*.
- Psychics' visions aren't always understandable at the time of the reading. Be patient. Because these readings can be longer-term predictions, they may require many years to manifest and make sense.
- Psychics can only see as clearly as the window through which they are looking. In other words, while psychics see visions of future events and even other dimensions, they can only interpret that information according to their own level of understanding in this realm. A smart psychic will say, "This is what I am seeing but I don't know what it means." Clients will usually interpret the reading according to the context of their current lives even though it may be an incorrect interpretation. Later, when the reading eventually applies as it was originally intended, the client will exclaim, "Oh! Now I understand what you meant in the reading."

So**, dear Unreadable,** do some research. Find a professional psychic who comes highly recommended and whom you can trust. Before a reading, don't be afraid to ask the important questions. Will you tell me any bad news? What do you believe about free will and destiny? What are your spiritual beliefs? Only commit to a session with someone who gives you a case of the "warm fuzzies." And let the seer know you are nervous and possibly blocked so that he or she can help you relax and unblock.

Once you find a psychic who is right for you, the information will flow and you will receive the guidance you are seeking. And if no one else can read you, listen to your own intuition. Or come and see me!

Remember, no matter what the reader says, what *you* choose to perceive and believe in your world is your choice, and *you* therefore, are always in charge of your own reality.

10

WHEN HOPE IS ALL WE HAVE

In the early afternoon heat, the art- and craft-filled fete shimmered in a colorful kaleidoscope of activity. Through the opening in my tented booth, my attention was caught by the tall white woman and the young, black-haired Native girl sitting in the warm sunshine on the green slope above the park. They sat together without communicating. As I watched them survey the people milling around the booths below them in the flatter area of the park, I sensed they were in the process of making a decision, and somehow I knew the decision involved me.

For the third year I was offering my psychic mini-sessions at this high-end annual craft sale. Crescent Park Fair was the only festival where I would do public readings as I usually avoided events where I might be perceived as a fortune-teller. However, at this exclusive exhibition the whole community turned out, and it was a chance to catch up with my existing local clientele—and a fun opportunity to meet new people.

I didn't have much time to ponder the two females as my next client plunked herself down on the chair in front of me and slapped her cash on the table. Fifteen minutes later when the reading was done and I came up for air, the Native girl and the woman were standing tentatively at the entrance to my booth.

"Come on in." I waved and smiled to ease their apparent apprehension.

"Can you read children?" the woman asked, inclining her head toward her companion.

"Absolutely." I beamed at the pre-teen girl. "But the readings are often more about potential," I said to comfort the parent more than the child. "Nothing nasty," I added, unaware of who I would be dealing with.

"Do you want me to stay?" the woman asked the girl.

In response, the girl just shrugged. I sensed she would have preferred the woman to leave but didn't know how to say so without offending. This feeling was confirmed when the woman squeezed her tall frame into one of my white plastic patio chairs and the girl's shoulders slumped in disappointment.

"What are your names?"

"This is Maya and my name is Sheila," the woman said. "Maya's been dying to have a reading with you," she added.

I smiled at Maya and took her delicate brown hands in mine. Almost instantly I felt a huge psychic thud in my own being, as if an elevator had crashed fourteen floors to the basement. This little girl had already experienced so much sadness in her short life. The pain was almost too much to bear. At the same time, I sensed an incredible strength in her, an innate wisdom, an old-soul energy. When this girl grew to be an adult, I sensed she would become someone powerful, perhaps even famous. I also knew that the brief reading I offered Maya in this casual park environment would not be sufficient. This was neither the time nor the place to discuss all she had to face. But at least I could begin the process.

"Wow! I'm glad you came to see me, Maya," I started. Her long, lank black hair fell forward to shade her face, but I could see the shy smile. "Oh, look, you're a dancer! A good one."

She glanced up at me then, her eyes also smiling. "I love to dance."

"And she's good," Sheila chipped in.

I guessed she was maybe twelve, small for her age physically but oh so mature, the kind of maturity that comes with having had too much happen too soon in life. "You are also psychic . . . wow . . . very, very psychic." I searched her face for signs of acceptance of this fact. She just nodded as if it were old news.

"You're quite the artist in other ways, too. I could see you writing, drawing, painting as well as dancing. But . . . something happened this year?"

"Her mother died," Sheila almost snapped.

"Oh . . . I'm so sorry, Maya." She cast her eyes down again, the sadness returning. "Was it the end of February?"

"Yes." Her eyes began to fill with tears. "February 27."

My heart went out to this little girl and her pain. I had to ask, "Did she die suddenly?"

Sheila nodded, remembering. Maya started to cry.

While I don't enjoy torturing my clients and causing them unnecessary pain, I needed to excavate something and set it free so she could heal. What I was also seeking was her question, the reason she wanted to see me.

"Did something happen one month before she died?" I addressed Maya but Sheila answered.

"Yes. She . . ." the older woman shot a glance at Maya and rubbed her eyes as if rubbing away the memory. *Tried to commit suicide?* I wanted to say out loud but spared Maya the pain of either the memory or the thought. "Maya's question is—is her Mum still around her?" Sheila asked, cutting to the chase. I understood.

"Let me see." I tuned in, struggling to keep my own tears down. Leaning forward and holding her hands in mine, I closed my eyes, hoping for her deceased mother to make herself known—through me—to her daughter who needed her so badly.

In my work, my agreement with my guides and my God is always to speak the truth. Sometimes that can be challenging, especially when I know that the person sitting in front of me is on the edge of her seat desperate for a certain answer. In this case, I really wanted to tell Maya that her Mum was watching over her, but sometimes, after a suicide, the spirit can get stuck in no-man's-land.

"It was very hard for your mother to stay in this life," I began, getting a trickle of the mother's essence. Maya's eyes reflected her struggle to absorb this information. The mother's vibration was becoming stronger. "She wants you to know that she can be a better mother to you in spirit than she could have been here. For some reason, it was just too hard for her in the physical."

Across the table, Sheila nodded agreement.

"Is my Mum around?" the girl asked again, the question heartbreakingly simple.

"Yes. Yes, she is." Now, finally, I could feel her presence and I could answer in truth and with conviction, "She's one of your angels."

Maya burst into tears then, leaning on the arm of the white plastic chair, her long, slim fingers swiping away her tears, an agonized timbre in her young sobs. I recognized the sound of gut-wrenching helplessness, the finality-of-death and the unable-to-turn-back-the-clock knowing of grief. Tears clouded my eyes and fell unbidden down my cheeks. Sheila, I noticed, also grabbed at the box of tissues on my table.

"I know," I said quietly. Taking Maya's limp hand in mine and remembering the excruciating pain of suddenly losing my best friend, lover, and husband-to-be, I added, "It hurts like hell."

I had lost *my* own mother when I was 17 but to a different kind of death. Insanity. Sheila sniffled and all three of us went for more tissues at once. We laughed then. I wanted to take this devastated little girl in my arms and just hold her. There was so much more there that I wanted to facilitate, but overstepping boundaries is not allowed. And this woman who was now very much in charge of Maya was protective of the child.

Despite her initial stern appearance, I could tell that Sheila had a big heart and sincerely wanted to help Maya feel better. But what was the connection between this woman and this girl? No blood relationship obviously. Foster mother? Aunt? Mother's friend?

"That's enough for now," Sheila said, wiping her face. "Maybe just some cards."

I nodded, already emotionally spent myself.

As if reading *my* mind, after I had read her cards, Maya asked quietly, "Will I see you again?" She had more questions, I sensed, about her psychic self. In that moment she saw me as a lifeline to that aspect of herself.

"Yes," I said, my heart melting again. "I hope so." I wasn't sure how her guardian felt about that. "Where do you live?"

"Kamloops," Sheila responded. "We're just visiting family this weekend."

That was a five-hour drive away. Too bad, I thought, *and not on my tour route at the moment.*

"If you give me your phone number," I said, handing her a small white index card and a pen, "I'll call you if I come to your area." The offer was a little lame. A visit there was possible but not in the immediate future.

"What about Bryson?" Sheila suddenly asked. I studied the older woman more closely then—the apricot shirt, her unkempt hair, her aura emitting an acknowledgment that she needed to pay more attention to her own body but she was too busy. I briefly pondered the many reasons people, men and women, don't give enough attention to their own bodies: too much busy-ness, low self-esteem, sexual abuse histories, health issues, or just a giving-up.

I tuned in again. "Bryson? . . . Is he Maya's brother? . . . And he's around 15?"

"Just about," Sheila responded, happy that I had his age right.

"Feels like he blames himself or he is angry, guilty about the death of his mother."

Sheila nodded, tears threatening to break loose again.

Poor babies, I thought. "I should probably see him, too," I said, leaning back in my chair. "He's in self-destruct mode . . . because he's feeling guilty and believes he deserves to be punished."

Maya uttered a sound of incredulity, perhaps because I had pinpointed her brother's motives so accurately.

"Certainly is!" the mother figure agreed.

"He's coming here today. I can bring him in," she offered.

"No." I got up. "It's not the right place."

We were out of time and the line-up outside my tent was growing. "Bryson may want to cry like his sister and he wouldn't allow himself to do that in front of a whole community." I handed Sheila my card. "Please . . . call me for a private appointment at my home. We'll make something happen."

That weekend, a friend of mine, Samantha, was staying with me. Though she is an artist of many genres and media, at that particular time she was in her angel-wing-making phase. As she showed me her latest beautiful works of art, I suddenly received a strong message that Maya needed to receive a pair of Samantha's angel wings. Perhaps it was her mother urging me to buy them as a sign that she was around Maya and watching over her? The wings would also remind Maya that her mother was in a much better, lighter place. Wings for me symbolize freedom, so maybe they would set mother and daughter free—to fly like angels, light and free of pain. Finding out if it was appropriate to send Maya this gift would be a good excuse to talk to Sheila again and find out more about Maya's history.

Later that week, I called Maya's guardian. The softness in Sheila's phone voice surprised me. People's facial expressions often belie their true essence.

"I wanted to buy a gift for Maya . . . a pair of angel wings. I felt her mother really wanted me to get them for her, but I wanted to make sure it was okay with you."

"Oh, she'd love them!"

"What colors do you think she would like? Green and red? Yellow and blue? Pink and purple?" I know how important color is. I had an inkling that Maya would choose the pink and purple but I wanted to get it right.

"The pink and purple," Sheila said without hesitation.

"How can I get the wings to you?" I asked. They were so fragile, I preferred not to entrust them to the mail.

Sheila already knew what to do. "We're coming to see you."

Oh, good. Had I underestimated the big-heartedness of this woman? She was so full of love for Maya and her brother. "Are you the aunt?" I ventured during our phone conversation, still not able to get an exact handle on her relationship to Maya.

"No. I'm Maya's Mum."

"Oh." *Now I was confused.* "But I thought . . . ?"

"I adopted Maya when she was just two, but we've kept an open relationship with her biological mother over the years."

"So can I ask you . . . did their mother commit suicide?"

She hesitated. "In a sense . . . yes. She drank herself to death."

"That's a form of wanting to kill yourself," I responded.

Sheila made a noise of acknowledgment.

"I felt a sense of self-destruction around her when I did Maya's reading. Sad."

"Yes . . . and you were right. Her Mum can probably be a better mother in spirit than when she was alive." She paused. "Maya sure was happy when you told her she was psychic, though. She thought she was crazy," Sheila continued. "She sees these three spirits all the time."

"Who are the spirits?"

"I'm not sure. She won't tell us, but they terrorize her."

After Sheila told me some of the psychic experiences that Maya was having, my heart went out to this young girl even more. What a lot for a young soul to bear! And I didn't even know the half of it yet.

"Maya should read my book," I suggested to Sheila. "Many of my readers have specifically said that my book assured them they weren't crazy."

"Oh, she's got the book." I liked this woman more and more. "I thought I would read it, too, and work through it with her."

Good idea. Though I had written the book primarily, I thought, for my client base of women from 25 to 60, nothing in the book would pose a threat to the mental health of teens. And several of my clients have told me that their teenagers purloined the book from their parents even before the adults had a chance to read it.

Sheila and I agreed on a date to bring the children to my house when I could give them both a spiritual healing. Or that's what I prayed for.

The following Monday on the dot of 10 a.m., I opened the door, surprised to see the mother *and* the father, Maya and her brother. Bryson was much smaller and darker than I had envisioned. His big brown eyes stared at me, and I could see from his narrow, hunched shoulders that he was holding his breath.

The family followed me up the stairs. I offered Sheila and her husband the option of staying while I did the reading—or going for a coffee. I was silently urging them to leave as I felt Maya really needed to talk to me alone.

"We'll sit here," Sheila responded, indicating the comfy couch in my living room, the same room in which I was going to read Maya.

Darn. "Okay."

Maya sat in the chair on the other side of my reading table in the alcove, not quite out of earshot of her parents, and we began.

I took my client's delicate hands again and repeated some of what I had seen before—a connection with New York when she was older, being a very strong energy, possibly becoming famous. "You have an older sister who doesn't live at home?"

Maya nodded. "Rachel."

"She's coming home to visit for a while," I said.

The adoptive mother let out a snort as if she would be surprised to see the girl.

Then to my relief, Maya's biological mother came through me again. I chose that moment to tell my young client that I had a gift which I felt her mother had urged me to give her, a set of angel wings. When I showed them to Maya, her face lit up with delight.

"They are a message from your mother," I said quietly, "to remind you that you can both be free now."

"I'll put them up on my bedroom wall," she announced gleefully.

Then I sensed the presence of a few spirits who were attached to Maya, but only two came forward, one small girl and another older man in a brown hat. When I asked her to let me know if one or both of them were hurting her in some way, she shook her head. "The girl is my friend. She makes me laugh." Maya smiled. But when I asked about the other spirit, she glanced uneasily over at her parents sitting on the couch and just shrugged. I knew that with them there she wouldn't tell me the truth.

So I did what I could under the circumstances. I gave her Psychic Protection Instructions 101 and taught her how to put the white light around her bed, her body, and her spirit at night before she went to sleep.

"Spirits are just like people," I told her. "If they aren't nice to you, just tell them to go away. The angel wings will also help you," I added. "Ask your angels, including your Mum, to come and protect you while you sleep."

At the end of the reading, Maya pulled some angel cards—*Breaking Free, Guardian Angel, and Freedom*—which just confirmed her mother's message and her reading.

While I knew that the session was helpful, it was also in some ways frustrating for me and I felt that my words were not quite enough for Maya. I had wanted to delve so much deeper into these spirit visitations with her, but the presence of her parents was inhibiting for both of us.

Bryson then took her place in the "victim's chair," as I jokingly call the client's seat. He was small for a 15-year-old but he also emanated a gregarious spirit. Some of his joviality, I suspected, was a thin disguise for his confusion and misplaced guilt about his mother's death. His long-deceased father was also around him in spirit, and I sensed he had also died from alcoholism. Bryson still missed him greatly.

"Do you have a blond-haired friend, Bryson?"

Bryson shrugged and nodded at the same time, not quite sure who I was talking about.

"Well, I don't want to say this boy is stupid exactly . . . ." At this, the whole family burst out laughing as they seemed to know *exactly* who I was talking about.

"He *is* stupid," Sheila piped up.

"I see him wanting to play on the railway tracks." I squeezed Bryson's hands for emphasis. "Please don't let him play on the tracks. It's not a very smart thing for him to do, and the outcome isn't good if he does."

Bryson nodded, absorbing the urgency of my message. "You're smarter than that, Bryson. You might go to the edge and push the envelope, but you stop yourself before it gets too dangerous." The boy's eyes flickered acknowledgment. "You also have a guardian angel who won't let you go too close to the edge. You could be a doctor if you wanted to."

"He wants to be in the NHL," his adoptive father interjected, letting me know they were still paying close attention to every word.

"You are definitely going to college," I continued. "When you are 18, I feel you will meet a girl who is very good for you, probably at college. She will mirror who you really are."

With Bryson, I also wanted to talk more about the death of his mother, but I could feel that the young man didn't want to open up to that can of worms with his adoptive parents sitting close by. When resistance is present, it's like a wall of thick energy that doesn't want to be touched. In this case, I respected it and backed away.

After the two readings, I sat in my leather chair in my living room, facing the whole family, two guardians and two children. While the adults seemed very caring, something big was missing from this jigsaw—the mystery of why Maya was being so tormented by spirits. I was frustrated at not having time alone with both children to dig deeper.

I could also understand the parents' concern. While they really didn't know me that well, they trusted me to a certain extent. And if I were a parent, would I entrust my young children to a psychic stranger? Probably not. Not wanting to embarrass Maya in front of her family, I tentatively probed about the spirits that followed her.

"They're just people without bodies," I counseled her. "They want to play with you. Just laugh at them. Get into the humor of it. It *does* take two to play the game. If you refuse to see them, they don't exist for you. They will get bored and think you're not fun anymore and leave. They'll go find someone else to bother."

Maya's face lit up with a smile reflecting my slightly jocular tone.

Then, in a gentle voice, the father, Victor, urged Maya to tell me about what the "bad" spirits had said to Jane, "the innocent girl spirit."

"Once Jane told me that—," Maya started. She stopped, remembering her own private nightmare, and began to sob, balling her hands into fists and rubbing her eyes, not wanting to see or hear what she had experienced.

"It's okay," I said, not wanting to cause her undue distress.

As Victor reached out gently to touch Maya on the arm, I noticed how she flinched at his effort of comfort as if to say, *Don't touch me*. I couldn't see why she would react so defensively to his care—except for the obvious. My antennae were always on alert for signs of sexual abuse. But this man was so gentle and caring, so intent on helping Maya, and his energy so "clean," that I pushed the thought from my mind. The abuser could be, or could have been, any male—her birth father, an uncle, a teacher, or worse . . . the spirit in the brown hat. It wouldn't have been the first time that I had heard of a spirit sexually assaulting a physical person.

"You are not crazy," I reassured Maya when she had rubbed her eyes dry. "If you're crazy, that makes me crazy, too." This didn't appear to reassure her but it did make Bryson smile.

"Maya told me that the spirits are mostly present at night, though sometimes during the day," the father continued.

"Does anyone else hear them?" I asked the family.

"Not usually," Sheila replied, "but I have heard noises like a flock of birds in her room and other strange noises coming from there." This piece of the puzzle began to ring a vague bell for me.

"Is it the house?" I wondered out loud.

"No," the father said. "We've moved several times, and they follow her wherever we go."

I had my own troubling theories as to why Maya was experiencing these visitations but it was just conjecture at this point. I needed more information, more facts. Something else, something deeper and bigger, was the real root of the problem, and it wasn't making itself known to me. Perhaps something or someone was blocking the information.

For the first time I could remember, I felt helpless, unable to suggest a course of action. Not that I hadn't referred others to all kinds of specialists before when I recognized they needed additional therapy. That's what I did about 25 per cent of the time. This guidance usually came easily and effortlessly. But with Maya . . . I would need to meditate on this case . . . or let it be for a while. Perhaps the answers would come.

If only I could get Maya alone . . . .

"We should leave and let Natasha get on," Sheila said, pulling herself out of my oh so comfortable armchair.

"Yes," I agreed remembering the list of phone calls I had yet to make. The children went downstairs and waited in the hallway while the adults stayed in my kitchen. The sound of giggling, the brother and sister making each other laugh, floated up from downstairs. It was music to my ears. *At least they have each other*, I thought, relieved.

"How long has she been seeing these spirits?" I directed my question to both parents.

Victor glanced at Sheila, frowning. "She talked about them as soon as she could speak. Two?"

Sheila nodded. She must have known I was perplexed. Before she spoke she cast a glance through the French sliding door and downstairs to make sure Maya was out of earshot. "She was abused when she was younger and . . . " she said quietly, as if we were in church, " . . . and she's had all these surgeries."

What! "What kind of surgeries? . . . Were they sexually invasive?" I asked softly.

Both parents nodded solemnly. "Oh, yes, all of them," Sheila affirmed.

My mind was grateful for the additional information but it took a while for me to absorb what Sheila was saying. *My god! Does the horror of this poor girl's life never end? Talk about a brave soul!* "No wonder I sensed something huge, and her need to be so strong. She had to be." Suddenly I had a psychic hit. "I wonder if these nasty energies are something to do with the surgeries?"

A light went on in Sheila's eyes.

"Do you think the spirits sexually assault her?" I asked.

"I think so," Sheila was reticent. "She won't say. Just that they do bad things."

"I do know people who have been raped by spirits," I told the parents. "If Maya has experienced so many invasions, perhaps that's the sexual violation I was feeling. And if she were psychic before, during, or after the surgeries, that would definitely be enough to disturb her etheric body, to rip holes in the fabric of her aura and make her vulnerable to low-life energies . . . ."

"It all makes sense," Victor said, shaking his head.

All three of us were silent. The parents mulled over their daughter's sad history. I was just plain stunned. Why would a little girl need so many surgeries at such a young age? Some sexual reconstruction due to damage? It didn't bear thinking about.

"I think Maya needs to see someone else but I'm not sure who yet," I said, feeling a little helpless at not being geographically closer to give her the psychic support I thought she needed. "Although I'm able to validate her psychic experiences, what I'm doing is merely a band-aid."

I knew that Maya needed to step into her power, but how could a 12-year-old Native girl simply do that after suffering all those invasive surgeries, the loss of both parents due to alcoholism, sexual abuse, and perhaps even spirit abuse, not to mention terrifying spirit visitations at night. It was a miracle that she was still here and still sane.

I paused for a while to assimilate this newest information, to put pieces of the jigsaw puzzle together. "Have you heard of a book called *The Bell Witch*?" I asked Sheila.

She shook her head.

"It's about the daughter of a minister in the 1800s. Poltergeist activity begins in and around the house and graduates to psychic attacks on various family members. Eventually, they discover that the daughter is being sexually abused by her minister father. The suppression of her rage shows up in not just the kinetic moving of furniture but also in these attacks, mainly against herself and then eventually against her father."

"I've been thinking along those lines . . ." Sheila said, leaning her tall frame against the kitchen counter.

"Let me think on it. If it's okay with you, I'll talk to some of my esteemed healer colleagues and let you know."

"Thank you," the couple said in unison as they moved toward the sliding kitchen door to the stairwell.

I followed them downstairs. Before they left, Maya threw herself at me, wanting a hug. Surprised and delighted, I held her tightly for a long time. I couldn't remember being so affected by a client, ever. She really was a special child. "It's going to be okay, sweetie," I said surprised at my own love for her and just wanting to hold onto her. "Just remember the white light protects you."

"I will," she whispered huskily into my shoulder and then skipping outside, holding her angel wings carefully above her shoulder, she climbed into the family's large green van.

Later that week, I was sitting at my dinner table with Helen and her partner, Ted, both of them psychologists who specialize in trauma. We were revisiting my first reading with Helen and marveling at how all my predictions, despite her initial cynicism, had come true—how she would expand into an international practice, start a foundation, and purchase an expansive new house with an all-round vista. Then I asked the question that had been plaguing me all week.

"Can I pick your psychologists' brains for a second?"

Though tired from their own practice, Helen and Ted graciously listened to Maya's long trauma-filled tale.

"What were all the surgeries on?" Helen asked.

"Her private parts. That's all I know."

"That's what I was getting," Ted said.

Both doctors instantly recognized the problem. "There would be a lot of trauma attached to those surgeries, and she would be vulnerable to sexual abuse by spirits," Ted commented.

"Yes, surgery is dangerous to the auric field, especially for psychics," I agreed. *Scalpels would definitely not be welcome in my aura,* I thought. "Can anything be done for Maya?"

"I can recommend someone who can help with the trauma," Helen answered. "But she should also go to see a shaman of her own culture. Do a sweat. I know someone not too far away, in Hope. I'll give you the numbers."

The next morning, clutching various telephone numbers, I called Sheila to relay my new information.

"My friends, who specialize in trauma counseling, or 'completion' as they call it, feel Maya needs to heal her trauma from the surgeries. And because her auric field has been violated through her surgeries, she's probably vulnerable to spiritual sexual abuse."

"Yes," Sheila simply agreed, as if she had known the truth all along but needed another party to identify it.

"Call this woman," I urged. "She's lives in your vicinity and she's lovely. I've met her."

"How do *you* know her?" Sheila enquired.

"She attended my psychic development workshop."

"So she will be able to help Maya with the spirits?" Sheila asked, still concerned.

"Yes, she's open to that definitely. And once the trauma is healed and the holes in Maya's aura are sealed, then the spirit manifestations will cease."

"But will this affect her psychic ability?" Sheila seemed concerned that Maya would lose the gift of seeing.

"No," I replied confidently. "Because she will be healing that hole in her aura, she will become a better, healthier psychic with strong boundaries. Then she will only attract the good spirits."

A long exhalation at the other end of the line conveyed Sheila's sense of relief.

"It's a beginning," I said, now confident that Maya would get the help she really needed and begin a journey of healing.

Two days later when I picked up the phone, I was surprised to hear Sheila's voice. "I need to tell you something about the angel wings." She sounded excited.

"What is it?"

"Rachel, Maya's sister, came back wanting to stay, just like you said in Maya's reading."

I just love to be right, I thought.

"But when Maya told Rachel that her Mum had bought the angel wings for her, Rachel said, 'Well, that makes sense.' Maya asked Rachel, 'Why?'—she's always hungry for any information about her mother—and Rachel told her, 'Mom always called you "my sweet baby angel."'"

As my skin prickled with the truth, I thanked Sheila for telling me.

So many clients and their stories disappear back into the ether, and it's the validations and feedback about my work that help me grow as a psychic.

"Did you call the trauma counselor?" I asked, anxious for Maya to begin her healing process.

"Yes, we called and we begin a set of sessions in two weeks."

Great!

"I want to stay in touch with you," Sheila continued.

"Yes," I agreed. "I feel such a connection with Maya and your family. Maybe in her past life as a shaman or medicine woman," I said, remembering some of her reading, "she healed me. And now I'm just returning the favor."

"Whatever it is, it's brought us all a sense of hope," Sheila responded, laughter in her voice now.

And sometimes, hope is all we have to keep us going on this journey we call life.

10 How Can I Protect My Psychic Child?

Dear Natasha,

My seven-year-old daughter wakes up screaming every night. She says the spirits taunt her. What can I do to protect her?

Dear Worried Mother,

I understand your concern. A child close to me has been visited by less-than-savory characters of the spirit variety. (See Chapter 8: "In The Psychic Net.") You *can* protect your psychic child, but first let me explain why she is attracting spirits.

For children to see spirits is not unusual. In fact, because most children are open to spirits, you could say that these children are all psychic. Some spirits may be their invisible friends, some their spiritual playmates, and others guardian angels protecting them until the child is accustomed to the earth plane. But as you know, less-than-angelic presences can also make appearances.

Spirits of people who have died suddenly—or who are still very attached to the earth plane—want to be seen. The unbounded openness that your psychic child is radiating shines like a search light in the spirit underworld. These lost spirits will be drawn to a psychic child like bugs to a light. Because misery loves company—and some of these spirits are miserable—they will then attempt to tease, taunt, and scare your child to make him or her as miserable as they are. Unfortunately, children don't know how to deal with these entities, and not surprisingly, feel powerless and terrorized.

As demonstrated in the previous story, children who have undergone emotional or physical traumas have often been exposed to the in-between realm and are sometimes vulnerable to lower vibrations of energy. While a psychic ability can be seen as a God-given gift, it can also be viewed as something to fear. Frightened adults in our childhood environments—often unwittingly, sometimes deliberately—kill off our inherently psychic talents. The psychic child—needing to belong and be accepted for the sake of his or her very survival—then conforms and shuts down on this ability to see. But more children than we know continue to see, feel, hear, or know extra-sensory data although they dare not share this information with their parents or siblings for fear of being estranged, penalized, or placed in a mental home! As these children mature, they learn to distrust their own minds. For psychic children, validating the psychic gift while teaching healthy boundaries is important.

Your child might believe that these spirits are just part of some recurring nightmare. These "in-between" spirits like to mess with children's heads. While your child may not be able to provide specific details of the "nightmares," she will be left with a disturbed feeling and definitely scared of she-doesn't-know-what.

The good news is that we can empower your psychic child, and all children, by giving them a stronger sense of self. Teach your child the following simple magical mind tools that she can call upon to protect herself physically and energetically.

1. Validate your child's experience—even if what she tells you is scary or doesn't make sense. You want your child to feel safe in sharing these events with you or her self-esteem may be crushed. If you don't validate her, not only will she not trust you again but she will be unable to trust herself for a long time. Even if you think it's just a nightmare, listen and confirm that her experience must have been scary.
2. Talk to a metaphysical expert. You *and* your child may also need someone who is psychically attuned to explain. For example, when your child talks of a spirit called Hamjee who shows her magic card tricks or of a sad little spirit girl who stands at the end of her bed, it is important that someone who understands her experience debrief her.
3. Do a spiritual cleansing of the bedroom and the rest of the house with dried sage (available at any metaphysical bookstore). Light the sage, and either with a feather or your hand, fan the smoke into the room and say a prayer that the room be filled with love and light only. Command any lower vibrational entities to leave and return to the light. As negative energy tends to get stuck in certain areas, also sweep the corners of the room with the sage and repeat the prayer. If you are uncomfortable with performing this ritual, ask a spiritual healer or minister for assistance.
4. Teach your child a visualization that makes her feel safe. If she believes on a deep level that she is protected, then she will be. Just before bedtime, tell your child to imagine that her bedroom is encased in a beautiful pyramid (or magical tent or forest) of protective white light that will stay there until she wakes. She can invite her guardian

angels to come into the pyramid and fill it with an even brighter light. If your child is too young to understand this concept, you can envision this pyramid of light on her behalf as you put her to bed at night. It works!

5. Affirm that she is in charge of her own space. Only those whom *she* chooses to enter her immediate space are allowed in. She has permission to tell the unwanted spirits, just like invasive people, to go away.
6. Know that the fundamental law of energy, like attracts like, applies here and in the spirit world. Encourage your child to focus on being safe and loved rather than being fearful. When psychically sensitive children are vulnerable to fear, they are more prone to psychic attacks. These attacks by low-life spirits often involve a feeling of being spun around faster and faster until we wake up feeling dizzy. While these "spinning" experiences occur in the dream state, the sensation can feel very real. If your psychically sensitive child is taught that she can decide who does and doesn't get close to her, and she is deeply comforted by loving and playful thoughts, then she will soon learn to be her own gatekeeper. Her strength will be her protection.
7. Allow your child—if she brings it up—to talk about her past lives with you. The best way you can react is to say, "Oh, really! And what happened next?" It will feel a little eerie. You might even get goose bumps—a sign of truth—but just go with it. The story might also trigger a deeper awareness for you.
8. Seek out more information. For example, Doreen Virtue's books (at www.angeltherapy.com), *The Care and Feeding of Indigo Children* and *The Crystal Children*, tell us about the phenomenon of psychic children who now inhabit the planet. According to Virtue, a brave band of spirits has agreed to come back to earth at this time to help us poor misguided souls through this major transformation. But Indigos and Crystals are more than psychically gifted. These little beings are highly intelligent and extremely psychic, and, due to their brilliance, have a very, very short attention span. For them childhood can be challenging, and consequently they can also make their parents' lives difficult. Often their behavior is confused with attention deficit hyperactive disorder, and they are medicated to numb their sensitivities! My theory is that some children who possess a high psychic IQ just might be suffering from excruciating boredom in this still primal, physical dimension. When consulting

with mothers of these supposed ADHD children, I have often sensed a higher spiritually evolved soul within their children and encouraged the parents to treat them as such. The high energy and seeming precociousness—instead of being suppressed with drugs—merely needs to be channeled into creativity.

So, **dear Worried Mother**, my friend with the psychic child was willing and courageous enough to take all the above steps. Her actions not only freed her daughter from unwanted nightly visitors but also empowered her psychic child with an innate strength and confidence in her own intuitiveness. We suspect that she is Indigo or Crystal as, since she was three years old and could talk, she has spoken of detailed past-life events. At five years of age she offered more metaphysically stimulating conversations than my own psychic colleagues, and at nine, she was giving amazingly accurate psychic readings. Whether your daughter is Indigo, Crystal, or psychic, be assured that by following the preceding steps, you and she can enjoy her fascinating and wonderful childhood, free of pesky spirits—both the living and the deceased varieties!

IF I SEE IT, I TELL IT

"Natasha, I need to talk to you!"

November rain was slashing my office window, so it was a perfect day for updating my client database and I had vowed that if the phone rang, I would not pick it up. But just ten minutes later the *dring-dring* interrupted my concentration. As I tuned into the ringing vibration, an overwhelming sense of urgency emanated from the black phone. I caved and grabbed the portable, and instantly recognized the voice of Nadia, a client from Victoria.

By her tone I knew the news wasn't good, but I asked anyway, "Nadia! How are you?"

"Terrible." She did indeed sound devastated. "I just got back from Italy. He didn't show up at the church! Why?"

Uh-oh. Italy? Church? I tried to recall Nadia's story, sifting through the client files in my brain and the ever-changing kaleidoscope of their biographies.

"Natasha," she pleaded again, "why?"

Oh, no. She wanted *me* to explain his absence. But I didn't know, and because I had been working in computer left-brain mode, my right brain was stubbornly refusing to click into intuitive gear. The only thing I could recall about that week in Victoria was that I had done 35 readings. Nadia's had been just one of them. "Remember our last reading?" she continued.

"Nadia, I'm sorry but I've done about 1,000 readings since then," I said. *Why do my clients test me like this?* I thought. I know their dramas are all-consuming to them, but theirs is just one reading to store in my memory bank. Reading between 10 and 50 clients per week and remembering each person's story is akin to attempting total recall of the dialogue of every movie I have ever watched. And it's not as if I am even consciously present during each reading. The information pours *through* me, not from me. I'm just a mouthpiece.

"Remind me," I suggested.

"You told me there would be a wedding before next Christmas. You were so convinced you said if it didn't happen, you would give up being a psychic."

Me and my big mouth.

"My wedding in Italy was all planned. It was going to be the event of the year in this small village where his parents live. I met them. He met my parents. The wedding was about to happen, but he didn't show up!" She paused, recalling the scene. "But you said something really crazy would take place at the wedding, like a Simon and Garfunkel song you said. What did you mean by that?"

I hit the search button in my mind. *Simon and Garfunkel song? Wedding? Crazy? Oh, yes.* "The wedding scene in *The Graduate*!"

"What?"

"*The Graduate.* That's the name of the movie. Paul Simon wrote the music for it. That's right. Boy has affair with Mrs. Robinson. Boy meets Girl and falls in love. Girl is Mrs. Robinson's daughter. Girl finds out about affair. Girl runs off to marry Rebound Boy. Just as she is about to say 'I do' to Rebound Boy, Boy bangs on church window and screams, 'Elaine, don't do it! I love you!' Girl leaves Rebound Boy standing at the altar aghast and elopes with Boy."

"Ohmigod," Nadia whispered, understanding dawning. "Maybe that's what happened, only I was Rebound Girl."

"Really?" Sometimes my own clairvoyance spooks me.

"He changed his mind at the last minute. Just like that. My wedding didn't happen."

I had an inkling of how cheated she must have felt. My own partner had died a week after proposing. "I'm so sorry, Nadia."

"Could you see that's what would happen?" Her question was an accusation.

"No, I didn't see that. I have an agreement with myself about my readings. What I see, I tell. But often things are shown to me symbolically that even *I* don't understand."

"Oh," she said and then, muttering almost to herself, she continued, "When you said it's like that song, I asked you what it meant exactly. And you just said, 'I don't know but it's crazy and it's happening at the wedding.'"

"I'm not shown everything," I explained. "I believe that my guides only show me what the client is ready to hear. And I'm not the judge of that. Think of me as watching a TV tuned to a certain channel. I'm merely reporting to you what appears on the screen. What I see is what I see." We both paused to reflect on my explanation.

"So what you see is also through your own perception?"

"*Exactly.* And trust me, that's also limited."

"I just needed to understand." She sounded resigned to her fate now. "You were so bang on with everything else." Normally I would have been pleased to get this kind of validation, but this time it didn't feel so good.

"Watch *The Graduate*," I suggested, trying to salvage something positive for Nadia to hang onto. "See if it triggers any deeper understanding for you."

After I hung up, it occurred to me that maybe Nadia's fiancé, on the rebound from another lost love when he had met her, wasn't able to handle the pressure from both families. As in the movie, he just couldn't go through with the wedding.

Both Nadia and I would have to live without ever really knowing.

11 Will You Tell Me Any Bad News?

Dear Natasha,

If I come to see you, will you tell me any bad news?

Dear Worried,

This common concern, expressed by many potential clients, is a question I believe all inquirers should ask of their psychics before consenting to have a reading. The person seeking the reading may not be strong enough to hear bad news, especially if he or she is emotionally vulnerable at the time. A vulnerable client might be inclined to surrender all his or her beliefs and power to a psychic. Negative information delivered in an insensitive way to such a client—and trust me, some psychics will blurt out bad news because they just don't care—could be damaging because the client is unable to process the data in an empowered, healthy manner.

My own abbreviated response to this "bad news" query has always been, "The question is not whether an experience is good or bad. An experience is just an experience. It is the meaning we give the experience and how we come to perceive it that we judge as good or bad." Negative events in the present can often turn into the greatest blessing of a person's life in the future. As Richard Bach states in his book *Illusions,* "There is no such thing as a problem without a gift for you in its hands. You seek problems because you need their gifts."

From the days of my earliest readings, I have intuitively understood the golden rule when relating what I see: To tell the truth and nothing but the truth. When a client asks me a question and I don't have an answer, I simply state, "I don't know." To make something up just to please the client or for me to say something in order to placate my own psychic ego is a big no-no. The information has to be authentic and from the divine source.

However, if I do see or feel something "bad," I also understand that I am not to exclaim, "Oh, look, I see you in a car accident!" or "Hey, guess what? You've got cancer!"

My purpose has always been to heal, so casting dire predictions and implanting negative beliefs into subconscious minds—especially when people are emotionally open and vulnerable—is dangerous. I realize that our beliefs create our reality and that my clients, therefore, could easily take my statements as truth and later manifest those events in their outer worlds.

Disempowering others, inadvertently or not—apart from being against everything I stand for—is just bad karma.

My first rule is: Do No Harm. At the same time, my job is to tell the truth. So I am *not* fulfilling my mission as a spiritual healer if I *do* see something the person needs to be aware of and do not impart that information. When stymied by disastrous visions, I silently call on my spirit guides, my angels, my client's guides, God, or the Archangel Michael and ask the question: *How can I communicate this information so my client is empowered?* Trusting that the negative data I am to communicate will be returned to me nicely packaged in a constructive format, I temporarily push the issue aside and get on with the rest of the reading. Sure enough, I soon hear channeled words tumbling out of my mouth conveying the negativity in such a gentle and positive way it almost sounds like a blessing. My witness self—the one who stands back and observes the reading—is often extremely impressed with the guidance. *Phew!* I think, *That sounded good. Thank you, angels.* My client's expression is usually one of relief, thoughtfulness, acceptance, sometimes even recognition. On some level, even if we are in denial, we *do* already know what's coming.

At other times, I am shown incongruous images such as elephants, ginger snaps, or buttons. I might also hear songs, or visit places and events that I can only describe to the client and say, "I don't know what this signifies but it's important I tell you this. The meaning will become clear to you at the right time, and then you will understand." Sometimes clients instantly understand the symbolic significance and burst into tears. Other times, the symbols are a mystery to both me and the client as was the case with Nadia. What I saw, I told. Sometimes, of course, because of karma or our own soul's need to repeat our painful experiences again and again until we heal them, we are not meant to avoid the experience but rather to learn the lesson. At the kernel of each lesson is a beautiful gift of enlightenment. Even if it takes years to acknowledge, the gift is always there.

I was obviously not meant to see that Nadia's wedding would be a non-event. But even if I had seen that drama and told her beforehand, she might have implanted the vision into her subconscious and then created that outcome for herself. Or, knowing that her plans would only end in heartbreak, she might not have gone through the process of having a relationship with this man and planning a marriage, thereby missing out on the lesson.

At the same time, I don't believe we have to learn through so much pain. Many of us are rising up to a much higher, more loving, more aware frequency. In that vibration, if we actively listen to our intuition, we can become more sensitized to the vibration of "iffy" energy so that we can sense impending downfalls before their actual manifestation. We are, in fact, becoming more psychic! We can now choose to change our thinking and raise our vibration long before the "bad" manifests in our outer world, and thereby exchange the negative outcome for a more harmonious and joyous result.

Now is that good news or is that good news?

12

THERE ARE NO VICTIMS

I could tell from Amanda's voice something was terribly wrong. "Could you come to my place and do a psychic party, Natasha?" Adopting a stiff-upper-lip tone, my client and friend was projecting joviality, but the strain filtered through.

"Are you okay?" I asked.

A long defeated sigh at the other end of the line conveyed more than the words that followed. "I'll tell you on Thursday when I see you," she said. "Why don't you come early and have dinner?"

On a sunny spring Thursday just before five o'clock, I pulled up in front of Amanda's sprawling Squamish home. The psychic party was due to commence at 7 p.m. Amanda had invited a small group of her 40-something-year-old friends, and I would be offering half-hour readings to each of them in a private room. Though psychic parties are normally fun and I was looking forward to it, I was also feeling a sense of dread.

The tantalizing aroma of garlic bread greeted me as I climbed onto a kitchen stool and watched from behind the bar as Amanda finalized preparations for a dinner of lasagna and salad.

With her back to me, she took the hot dish out of the oven and threw the oven mitt on the kitchen counter, as if defeated by the lasagna. "So what's up?" I asked her.

She turned, her face suddenly crumpling as all the air left her body. For the first time, I noticed she had shed a lot of weight. Usually I would have complimented her on her new svelte figure but I could see the pounds had melted from some terrible stress.

Amanda's large, sad brown eyes glistened with tears. "It's Terri, my daughter . . . ."

I waited. As she took a wide-bladed knife out of the drawer and sliced angrily into the cheesy crust of the lasagna, she told me the story.

"In February, my oldest daughter, Terri, met this man in a club." Amanda passed me a plate with an ample serving of pasta. "At first, she didn't seem interested," she said. "But then he called her for three days in a row and now, two months later, she's *mesmerized* by him." Amanda's shoulders sagged in despair as she dumped a miniscule serving of food onto her own plate. "He's known to the police for pimping, drug-dealing, and violence against women." She sank onto the stool next to me and took a napkin from the basket. "He's done terrible things."

Amanda's contorted expression conveyed the excruciating pain she was in. Putting her story into words, I could see, made her nightmare ever more real. Plagued by grief, she was desperate to get her daughter back.

"'Scumbag' is too nice a term for him!" She continued, scowling as she violently tossed the salad. "I just don't understand. Terri has always been the strong one, the one to tell her friends that *their* boyfriends aren't good enough. She's only 21, and now here *she* is under this guy's spell." She shook her head. "That's all I can say, she must be under his spell. She's totally in love . . . . And he's murdered people!"

"Ohmigod!" *I sure hope he isn't going to drop in for dinner.*

As I glanced around the sunny and pristinely clean home, I saw no hint of anything remotely sleazy. Amanda's upbringing, energy, and values I recognized, like mine, as being middle-class. This mother and her family represented the height of respectability. My background was similar and so I understood her shock and disbelief. *Why had Terri attracted someone of such a low vibration?*

"Actually, I didn't want to tell you this before you did the reading with her," she whispered, frowning. "Will it make a difference?"

"No. Not really. I see what I see," I told her. "It will just help me understand *what* I'm seeing." While this statement would prove correct, it would still take much longer than usual for me to comprehend.

"Has anything major happened to Terri to lower her self-esteem?" I instantly thought of rape or some other equally heinous trauma.

Amanda's eyes darted from side to side as she searched her databank of information. "No." She shrugged. "Nothing that I know of."

Like attracts like, I thought. Something must have created an opening in Terri's aura, a lowering of her vibration, to allow this dark force into the chink of an otherwise light being. Something *must* have happened. Unless this fall from grace had been part of Terri's soul agreement . . . ?

After dinner, Carol, Amanda's friend and one of the women to be read, entered the kitchen. As soon as she sat down, she launched into an interrogation about my life as a psychic. "Do you ever use ouija boards, Natasha?"

"I wouldn't touch a ouija board with a ten-foot barge pole," I stated firmly.

"Oh, they're fine," Amanda said, almost scoffing at my fear, her back to me as she poured after-dinner coffee.

"You have to know what you're doing with them," I insisted.

"Well, we had a séance in January and there were no problems," Amanda announced.

"You did?"

"Yes." Amanda glanced up.

Uh-oh.

"Was Terri there?" I asked, my heart beating faster for no apparent reason.

Amanda frowned. "Yes, yes, she was. Why? . . . Oh, you don't think . . . ?" Her consternation reflected my concern.

"And nothing untoward happened?" I asked.

"No." Amanda passed me a big mug of coffee. Her hand, I noticed, wasn't too steady now.

"No slamming of doors, spinning of glasses, lights flickering? No nightmares or other disturbances in the house afterward? Nothing like that?"

Still Amanda shook her head. "No, it was fine. Really."

I wasn't so sure it was "fine," but I didn't want to push the point with Terri's mother until I had met and read Terri. I had heard many a tale of possession of the uninitiated after an innocent little ouija board session. Low-life spirits roam the earth just searching to reinhabit a physical body through which they can wreak their revenge for an untimely death or other unresolved issue. Séances are perfect opportunities for lost souls to find hosts in unsuspecting and uneducated participants.

Suddenly, a tall, athletic girl with long, straight, blonde hair bounced into the kitchen.

Amanda inhaled. "This is Terri, Natasha."

Just as her mother had described her, Terri was the epitome of a soon-to-be-successful young woman. She smiled and offered her hand. I shook it while attempting to disguise my shock because the story did not match the clean energy of this person before me.

"Are you ready for your reading?" I asked her.

"Sure." She shrugged and followed me into the small office where I was to do the sessions.

I was intrigued by Terri's energy. While her aura didn't appear to be disturbed, something about her was closed, distant, if not absent. I couldn't decide if she was grounded or very guarded. The veneer was practiced and smooth and solid, like a wall that was challenging to see beyond. Psychic readings are, after all, a two-way street between client and reader. However, I did get a strong sense of a presence in and around her.

"Have you ever had the feeling that you've been a prostitute in a past life?" was one of my first questions.

She shook her head and gave me a blank stare.

"Well, I sense," I persisted, "that you might have been a hooker and that your life was cut short. You were possibly murdered or you died suddenly. And you were three months pregnant. I now feel you've come back in part to finish something off."

Terri shrugged. Nothing was hitting home, or she didn't want to acknowledge the truth.

"Your new relationship has come at this time," I told her, "because it has something to do with this past life. In some way, you have come together with Jason to finish something."

"Oh, yes, he's amazing," Terri cooed.

So I hear, I thought.

For the first time her eyes lit up. She came alive and spoke of him as if he were every woman's knight in shining armor.

"I think you'll be moving twice," I continued, "living somewhere for a short time and then moving again." *I hope it isn't jail.*

She frowned.

"I also see you talking to the police. You are all right but . . . an incident has occurred that is shocking to you." The scene of Jason violently beating someone unfolded in my head. I saw that when Terri witnessed this violence, she would suddenly snap out of her spell with him and then help the police arrest him. Again she stared at me expressionless. Then something, some energy, flitted across her face. I wondered if she were in a trance of some kind.

What I didn't tell her was that her association with Jason was short-lived. The relationship would last as long as she wanted it to, no matter what I told her. And while this man was decidedly unhealthy for her, their connection was something Terri had to experience as part of her karma as a hooker.

"You're protected," I told her seeing that, surprisingly, no physical harm would come to her.

"I've always felt that," she agreed.

"But drugs are being offered to you. Don't take them . . . not just for the obvious reasons . . . but they're dangerous, not pure."

Terri's response was another vacant stare. I sensed she had not started into the drugs, but she would be surrounded by them soon and, as happens with so many, she would succumb to peer pressure.

Was any of this information registering? Terri's eyes didn't react in understanding, agreement, or resistance. *The lights are on but no one is home,* I thought. Months would elapse before I fully understood why.

Later in the evening after Terri had left and all the other women, clutching their taped sessions, had gone home, Amanda offered me a comfy seat in her open-plan living room. She then plied me with herbal tea and questions about Terri. I reassured her without betraying her daughter's—and my client's—confidences that I saw this unhealthy relationship not lasting long. "However, Amanda," I stressed, "this part of her life is something she has to do. It's part of her fate."

"But why?" The deeply etched lines on Amanda's face hinted at the pain of her sleepless nights.

I could not know, not having been a birth mother, exactly what she was going through. Sometimes, life's tragedies just do not make sense . . . at the time anyway.

"It's her soul agreement," I said. "She's come back to finish something off—her life as a hooker."

Amanda jolted in her chair. "Did you tell her that?"

"Yes."

"And how did she react?"

"She didn't really."

Terri's story would not make sense to either of us for a while.

Over the next few months, I kept abreast of Terri's drama through Amanda. The attraction between Terri and her very-bad-boy wasn't as short-lived as both Amanda and I had hoped, not by a long shot. Almost a year later, however, as I was writing a chapter in my first book, the truth of Terri's story suddenly hit me.

I called Amanda. "Let's meet for lunch."

A few days later in Vancouver, as she and I sat in a small café overlooking a sunny, sparkling ocean, I said, "You know how I told you that I sensed Terri was a hooker in a past life?"

"Yes . . . ."

"Well, that's not the whole truth." I paused as I asked for divine guidance to help me communicate what I was about to say. "I also saw that this hooker was three or four months pregnant and was murdered by her pimp boyfriend. Now I think . . ."

Amanda put down her fork as I hesitantly delivered the bad news.

". . . that Terri wasn't a hooker in a past life but that *now* she is actually *possessed* . . . by the hooker. And that Jason is the man who murdered her and her fetus. She's come back to wreak her revenge."

To my great relief, Amanda sat back in her chair and exhaled as if I had just announced that her nightmare was all over.

"You know that's the only thing that makes sense," she said. "I spoke to her this morning and it doesn't even sound like her. She's so hard."

"What I keep going back to is that something must have happened to bring Terri down to his level, a weakening in her aura. If she was present at the séance, it probably opened up something on that vibration."

"She always did like to live on the edge, always pushing the envelope." Did Amanda realize she was talking about her daughter in the past tense? "What should we do?" she asked, a mixture of desperation and returning hope.

"We could try for an exorcism," I suggested.

"But she's not here, she's in Montreal."

"We can do it remotely. But I have to tell you," I added, "that I'm not comfortable dealing with that kind of energy. Happy healing is more my style, so I leave exorcisms to the experts."

"Then who?"

"I'll find someone through my network," I assured Amanda.

We both sat in silence for a while, sipping our coffees.

"But at some point," I told her, "Terri will entrap the boyfriend. Mark my words. I don't know when, but she will. That's what the hooker came back to do, and she's using Terri's body as a vehicle."

I sat back and sipped my coffee, glancing out at the sun on a glistening ocean, sailboats bobbing in the harbor. Such an innocent scene. "There are no victims," I added. "This possession is an agreement between the host, Terri, and the possessing spirit. Terri will probably host the spirit of this hooker until in some way she has wreaked her revenge on Jason for her death and the death of her baby. Only then will the karma be complete and the hooker leave."

"God, it's awful," Amanda shook her head in disbelief.

I wished I didn't feel so powerless to give Amanda more relief from this nightmare, but she did seem a little more resigned to my interpretation of events. "I will find someone who can do a remote exorcism for Terri, if and when she's ready. Be warned, even an exorcism may not work unless Terri and the hooker are ready and willing to forgive Jason. In the meantime, all we can do is pray for Terri's speedy return."

12 Why Are Ouija Boards Dangerous?

Dear Natasha,

Why are we told never to play with ouija boards? Are they really dangerous?

Dear Ouija Enquirer,

My advice in a nutshell? Unless you are psychically trained, *don't* use them, at least without professional help. Personally, I would not have one in my house.

The word "ouija" comes from the French *oui* and German *ja*, both meaning Yes. Perhaps because they have been in existence for centuries as a way of communing with the deceased and divining the future, users of the board still think of them as some kind of game. As you can surmise from the previous story, playing with the ouija board is no game.

What happens when a group of unsuspecting enquirers gathers around a ouija board and starts asking questions of the spirit world is akin to living in a bad part of town, flinging open the front door, and inviting everyone, including thieves, drug dealers, and murderers, into your home. If that's what you want to do, go ahead. But know this: living criminals are far easier to get rid of than dead low-lifes.

The objects we wear and use not only carry our energy but can also attract other "attachments." The ouija has only one purpose—to attract and communicate with dead people. The danger is that the board could also carry residue energy attached from past séances. This residue might include not only the energy of previous users but also of former nasty spirit visitors.

As we already know, when people die who are not at peace, they cling to the earth plane. Sometimes these disturbed spirits do not accept their own death and want to be back in a physical body—any physical body—so they can work out their unresolved issues. They refuse to go to the light because they don't believe in it, or they don't believe they deserve to go to "heaven." These low-lifes are just waiting for the psychically vulnerable to set up the ouija board and open that portal so they can step back into the physical realm.

I have been accused of exaggerating the dangers of ouija boards, but possession happens more often than we realize. Unlike the movie *The Exorcist,* a not so nice spirit taking up residence in your body isn't always obvious. As in the previous story, the possession was more subtle although in the end no less dramatic. Some cultures believe that even illness is a form of possession by an evil spirit. Perhaps they are right.

Once these low-lifes enter your home—or your physical body—they don't want to leave. Because you are vulnerable and you don't know what or whom you are dealing with, they can have a lot of fun terrorizing you and making your life, like theirs, pure hell. You will then need your own exorcist to have them evicted.

The dysfunctional spirit doesn't always have to inhabit your body. Sometimes they choose to merely attach and hang around in your aura. These attachments could show up after using a ouija board and could be the spirits of relatives, friends, or strangers with whom you share an emotional but partially negative attachment. They tend to "stick" to you until you become aware of them and the issues are resolved by your healing your guilt or merely clearing the attachment. Unless you are sensitized to attachments, you might not immediately be aware of their presence. Some of these beings are like vampires, feeding off your energy until eventually you become conscious of a heaviness in your energy, like a flu infection. Then you need to sage yourself and/or visit someone who can help you disentangle from those energies.

Whether the spirit intends to possess you or attach to you, the same laws of Universal energy apply: like attracts like, that is similar energies seek each other; and complementary energies attract, that is, one part seeks the other part to create the whole. In order for a spirit to be attracted to your energy, therefore, your emotional issues will be similar or complementary to theirs. There are no victims. You might be emitting a psychic invitation to that spirit, even on an unconscious level, to share the possession/attachment experience so that you both may heal an unresolved issue . . . eventually.

So, **dear Ouija Enquirer**, if you do insist on having a séance and using a ouija board, for your own protection please invite a professional spiritual facilitator whether that person be a psychic, a spirit medium, or a minister. The facilitator will probably first cleanse the board of past energies, enclose the circle in protective white light, and, while intoning spiritual prayers and blessings, invite only the highest energies to enter the portal. Good spirits are around, too, and they just might like to have a wee chat. Having a loving conversation with the good guys in the higher realms is a wonderful thing. You will know them by their incredible lightness of being.

PRESIDENTIAL VALIDATION

"Can you do it?" Jamie asked.

"Love to," I responded, checking my diary and making sure I was free. I was being hired for another Playtime Inc. event where for two hours I would give five-minute readings to as many clients as could be fitted into such a short space of time.

At these corporate dinners, one or two hired psychics would be positioned at tables near the clients in the restaurant. If the spirits moved them to do so, before, during, or after their dinner, the attendees—whether insurance agents, doctors, technical experts, or communication gurus—would come over to the psychics for a short reading. Because of the popularity of these events, I usually had to extend by one or two hours and I decided to ask another psychic, Joan, a Tarot reader, to assist me.

On that early summer's eve, in the roof garden at the Chateau Whistler Hotel, the sunlight filtered in through the large, latticed, ivy-draped windows, softening the early dusk light. We laid out our psychic paraphernalia on our respective tables, mine to the left of the French-doored entrance, Joan's to the right, so that we would be the first people the guests saw as they entered.

And soon they began drifting in, already rosy-cheeked and giggling from cocktails downstairs in the grand but still cozy Mallard Bar.

"Oh. What fun!" exclaimed one woman in a long, black, rhinestone-studded dress. "Psychics!"

Yes, I thought. *It is fun, until we hit the nail on the head.* Then the client's jaw drops, she sits up, pulls closer, and pays attention.

Soon the rest of the group ambled in. The men glanced in our direction. By their nervous reactions, we could see that they were registering what we were doing there, waiting for willing victims at our purple-sequined cloth-covered tables. *Oh, no! Psychics!*

I smiled to myself as they quickly fixed their blank stares forward, deciding that if they ignored us, we didn't exist. The women, meanwhile, appeared either delighted, curious, or indifferent. With these groups I never quite knew what the reaction would be. Presumably because someone had requested our services, believers walked amongst them. But any large gathering also harbors doubters.

Almost immediately women started coming over to my table, some shyly, some as if they were sneaking off from the group to do something naughty. Some were excited, plunking themselves down and thrusting their flattened, opened palms at me.

In a five-minute reading, I have to get to the heart of the matter quickly. The time constraint necessitates intense concentration. Of course, some people are easier to read than others, but if the client is open to receive my information, tuning in is akin to throwing a door wide open and being able to see everything. The pictures appear instantly as if they are just waiting to be viewed. If I don't have to excavate the information, this willingness to be seen makes my life as a psychic so much easier.

When our allotted time drew to a close, a line-up was still forming at my table. As I expected—I am psychic after all—a representative of the company approached me and asked whether Joan and I would be willing to extend by an extra hour. These corporate groups often underestimate how popular these readings are, or perhaps we just surprise them with our accuracy. My colleague and I had already agreed to stay if asked. I nodded agreement.

Toward the end of the evening, a young blonde-haired woman in a wheelchair propelled herself over to me. After I shifted to a comfortable position around my table where I could easily read her hands, we began. She was, I guessed, somewhere in her mid-thirties. Standing, she would have been tall. Even now, she sat erect in her chair. I learned that in her 20s she had survived a bad diving accident that had left her a quadriplegic. The intelligence in the woman's eyes was almost startling. I supposed, as with any restriction in our being, our other senses tend to become stronger in compensation, a natural balancing act. From behind the prison of her immobilized body, her eyes took in everything. I could imagine that since her accident she had lived lifetimes in her head. Her hands did not respond easily to the messages from her brain so I gently took her long, slightly clawed fingers and spread them wide.

I closed my own eyes, holding and stroking her hands, feeling with my thumb the center of her hand, her palm chakra. As I did with all my clients, I stroked the various mounts in her palm and was able to tune in to where the tension was held, where the energy was stuck, and where it flowed. I had expected to feel a lot of tightness in the Mount of Mercury, a sign of frustration, but I was pleasantly surprised to discover that this woman was amazingly accepting of her fate.

"Oh!" I gasped out loud.

"What?" The woman asked softly, curious.

"May I ask how old you are?"

"Thirty-six."

"Well, I can always be wrong but I'm being shown this vision that when you're forty years old, you will be walking."

Her eyes barely registered these words, and an almost weary expression drifted across her face as if she had been made a thousand promises and not one had come true.

I shivered as the goose bumps spread across my back and down my arms. Goosebumps are always a sign for me of truth, of imminent manifestation.

"Though I haven't read this anywhere, I feel that some researchers in the medical community are in the process of inventing tiny micro-computers. I see them placed, implanted, all the way down your spine. These microchips are doing the work of your nervous system, allowing you to walk, to function normally."

While I was brimming over with excitement for her, quivering with the wonders of technology that enabled humankind to mimic the human machine, she stared blankly toward somewhere just beyond my right shoulder.

"By forty, you'll be walking," I repeated, just to make sure she understood me.

Still the blank stare.

Maybe she didn't dare to believe. Why should she? To her, perhaps I was just some crazy psychic who was telling her what she so badly wanted to hear. And sometimes, unconsciously, people don't want to get better. The pay-offs for remaining a victim are sometimes greater than the freedom of responsibility. But I knew, *I knew* this recovery would happen. As my five-year old psychic niece responded whenever she was asked how she was able to predict something, "Oh, I just knowed it." And even as I watched this woman navigate her chair back to her table while

I was gathering up my psychic accoutrements, I wondered if she would even entertain my prediction.

Maybe because I see a lot of clients and peer into a lot of souls, especially during these corporate events, I allow the readings to slide off me like water off a duck's back. But some people and their readings stay with me. So it was with this woman's reading.

Only a month later, I was at home one evening, busy on the computer in my office. I took a break and strolled through the living room to the kitchen to make myself a cup of tea. My partner was taking in President Clinton's State of the Union address on television. I knew I was meant to hear what he said next.

". . . Scientists are also working on . . . ," I stopped in front of the TV as the President's voice boomed into our living room, his finger stabbing at the audience and his eyes narrowing with familiar intensity, "—and listen to this—microchips that would actually directly stimulate damaged spinal cords in a way that could allow people now paralyzed to stand up and walk."

I stopped, tea cup in hand and inhaled.

His audience applauded enthusiastically as if this invention were President Clinton's own.

"See! See!" I told my partner excitedly.

"What?"

"I was right."

"You're always right." He smiled, a hint of sarcasm in his voice. He obviously didn't know what I was talking about, and neither had the woman in the wheelchair. I just hoped she was watching the address. If she didn't believe me, maybe she would believe the President of the United States.

13 Is My Psychic Right or Is She Crazy?

Dear Natasha,

I just went to see a psychic who forecast some outrageous things in my future. I would like to think she's right but I wonder if she's crazy. How can I know whether her visions are accurate?

Dear Doubtful,

Funny you should ask that! Many of my own clients, when I announce my predictions, will peer at me with suspicion, cynicism, and outright disbelief in their eyes. Just as with the client in the previous story, I don't have to be psychic to know what they are thinking: I can see it in their eyes—*Natasha is nuts!* My standard responses to their expressions of disbelief are: a) in spite of my predictions, you won't do anything you don't want to do; b) my predictions could be wrong because perhaps I am misinterpreting the energy; or c) you have free will so you could change the outcome and/or the timing of the outcome.

While the modi operandi of psychics vary greatly, the psychic's images, just like dreams, should reveal something *you don't know,* some truth you were previously not able or willing to see for yourself. It might help you to discern whether you can trust your clairvoyant—or not—if you understand how I, as just one psychic, tune in.

I work on the premise that the experiences of our past, present, and future are not separated by time, just space. We humans have used the measurement of time to quantify these spaces until we have come to believe that time—rather than space—is our master. What psychics see, therefore, are not events in the future but potential manifestations out there in space, still in the ether. The events might materialize and touch us or they might just stay in etheric form and pass us by. The choice is ours. Whether we attract or repel the potential manifestations is decided by what we believe is possible, what we *think* we deserve, and what is already written into our soul agreements. Consequently, an event that you might think is out there in your future actually already potentially exists, even though it has yet to materialize in your immediate physical world. The psychic gift is to be able to see into the future—into the ether—and recognize these potential manifestations.

Regardless of whether the information is positive or negative or whether the psychic is considered good or bad, many people do not trust what the psychic sees. This lack of trust in the information or in the psychic might arise because these clients are skeptical about deserving the good coming their way and consequently refute what the reading offers.

Human nature being what it is, my clients will often overlay their own meaning onto my reading despite my insistence on what the guidance is telling them. Because they do not have the vantage point to see into their own futures, they will attempt to make my words and visions fit *their* current reality and limited perceptions.Their understanding of the reading, however, often changes when—at the right time—the future situation corresponds with my prediction. Two weeks, six months, or five years after a reading, I will frequently hear the words, "Natasha, *now* I understand what you meant!" *Praise the Lord!*

As a seasoned psychic, I have long accepted the fact that I am not always privy to the meaning of my own readings. Some of the images I see puzzle me but are understood by my client. For example, I might see the image of a banana peel. Once I report it to the client, she might say, "Oh, that's a joke my late father and I shared," thus validating a contact message from the spirit world.

But if the information does not resonate with either my client or myself, I offer a wider interpretation of the energy—both in literal and symbolic terms. For example, if I see my client crashing her vehicle into a brick wall, I might interpret it as a literal warning about a car accident or perhaps as a metaphorical warning about a "crashing" of some sort in her life. Either way, it is a warning for her to slow down, review the path she is on, and make some adjustments.

While I cannot speak for the validity of your psychic's message, I would suspect that, like myself, she is *not* making up these images that present, outrageous as they may seem to you. Feelings, visions, and words appear in the psychic's mind. Our job is simply to report those messages.

Speaking only for myself, if I start to analyze, judge, or doubt the message, then my ego is getting in the way of a higher spiritual truth. As a conduit, my value is simply in being the messenger of whatever comes through. If the meaning is made apparent, then, of course, I convey it to the client. But I also trust that, when I don't understand the message at the time of the reading, comprehension will dawn for the client when the time is right and when he/she is ready to receive that enlightenment.

If I were to read you, for example, I would inform you of what I am seeing, no matter how outrageous you might think it is. While some events are 100 percent certain to transpire—because those events are part of your soul agreement—other happenings are "maybes" and I would tell you so. You always have free will and can choose to accept or reject the event. My job is to speak the truth, offering a deeper understanding of the energy influences surrounding you at the time so you can make informed choices with your free will and be empowered to create your own future.

In the process of a reading, as I access your subconscious where you hold your beliefs, I would be able to discern what blocks are in the way of your higher good. Your soul agreement and your purpose for this lifetime would also be apparent, as well as your challenges and gifts. Based on those revelations, you would then be aware of all that is available to you, outrageous or not.

As a psychic, I believe it is important for me not to be deterred by being *seen* as right or wrong, crazy or sane. My goal is to empower, heal, and support my clients in realizing their greatness on their spiritual journey. Predicting a positive future is easy because the goal of our evolution is joy. Our journey is always about growth toward that end. Of course, we can have some major challenges along the way, but if I see those, either I steer my clients away from disaster thinking or I explain those events in the context of growth so that they can keep moving forward with hope and courage.

So, **dear Doubtful,** I predict that you have some options.

One option is to think of your psychic as crazy, hallucinatory, and perhaps belonging in a straightjacket.

Another option is to embrace the idea that maybe, just maybe, your ego is telling you these predictions are outrageous because the ego consciousness typically tends to talk us out of our greatness to keep us small. Nevertheless, these prognostications might be the truth of your higher destiny.

A third option is take the higher path and choose to believe you are in charge of your own future. If the future your psychic portrayed for you happens to be to your liking, why not choose to believe it, embrace that potential, and envision that magical future out there in the ether getting closer and closer and closer . . . until it becomes your current reality?

Sometimes the truth *is* outrageous—and magical!

SAVED BY THE WHITE LIGHT

It was January and the second night of my trip to Toronto. Before descending into the land of nod, I said my prayers of gratitude for everything and everyone in my life. I also sent healing light to the friends and clients I knew who needed it. While away from my partner, Neville, and my "stepchildren"—Tom, eleven, Alexis, eight, and Kyle, seven—I always imagined them individually protected in bubbles of white light. But this night, something was wrong.

Being the proverbial free spirit, I had always accepted traveling to other destinations as an integral aspect of my psychic business. Then I met and fell in love with Neville and inherited his three young children as my new family. Now leaving them, even for a few days, was hard. I was normally comforted by the knowledge that their father would take good care of them. And so I didn't understand the vision I was having.

Tom's white bubble was cracked, and my static vision of him standing in our living room suddenly mutated and came alive. I watched surprised as a mental picture of him doubling over, a grimace of extreme pain on his young face, etched itself in my mind. He was clutching his right side. Then it came to me. Appendicitis! Neville, who was standing in the background, was dismissing his son's cries of pain.

Before I had left on my trip, Tom had not complained of any stomach problems, so when I spoke to the children's father on the phone the following day, I asked him, "Is Tom okay?"

"Yep, he's fine," Neville responded, never one to elaborate with details.

"Well . . . ," I faltered, not sure how he would take my psychic vision, "if he starts complaining of stomach pains, you *must* get him to the hospital straight away because it will be appendicitis." My concern was that

I wouldn't be there and, as in my vision, Neville would not realize the urgency of the situation.

"Uh-huh," he grunted, sounding unsure whether to believe me or humor me.

"If you don't take him straight away," I stressed, "it could burst."

I waited for a response but heard only silence at the other end.

After my return the next day, I found a quiet moment to speak with Tom as he lay on the couch watching television.

"Tom?"

"Hmmm?"

I thought carefully how I should phrase the question as I didn't want to implant the idea of appendicitis in his mind and have him create it. "You don't have any stomach pains, do you?"

"Sometimes," he answered immediately, looking mildly surprised at my knowing.

"You do?" After twenty-five years of readings, I was still startled when one of my psychic visions was validated. "Where?"

Tom thought for a moment and then put his hand on the right side of his abdomen.

"Here."

"Are they sharp pains or just aches?"

Tom grimaced. "Sometimes it's sharp."

Uh-oh. "Well, if they get any worse, be sure to let me or your Dad know straight away." In this family, the boys didn't often express their feelings, and Tom especially liked to keep his problems to himself. "Okay?" I urged.

"'Kay," he muttered, returning his gaze to the idiot box, apparently not even curious as to why I had enquired about his periodic stomach problems in the first place.

When I relayed the conversation to Neville, he gave me a distant, mildly quizzical look. Was he unnerved that my vision was predictive or unnerved because psychics really *do* predict? While Neville totally supported me in my spiritual healing work, saying, "I think what you do is great," he was more comfortable when I counseled other people. As far as he and his children were concerned, I got the feeling that he preferred me to leave them out of the psychic loop. Still, I took the precaution of letting Tom's mother know. While Diane didn't exactly embrace my psychic abilities, she didn't pooh-pooh them either.

Then one Sunday in March, six weeks later, Diane took Tom out for the day. When she dropped him off in time for dinner, Neville was busy in the kitchen and I was folding laundry in the bedroom. As soon as I walked into the living room, I saw that Tom's normally pinkish complexion was deathly white. He was doubled over in pain and clutching his side. Tears were sliding down his pale cheeks.

"Tom, what's the matter?" I asked. The scene was eerily familiar, the question redundant.

"I've had stomach pains all day." His gentle blue eyes were clouded with anguish. "Mum wouldn't take me to the doctor."

"We have to get him to the hospital," I called calmly but firmly across to Neville where he stood over the stove, poking a large pot of pasta with a wooden spoon. His body stiffened and he just shrugged. "He'll be okay," he muttered, obviously displeased. Then inclining his head toward Tom, he commanded, "Go and lie down."

I fought to suppress my own vague sense of panic. "But Neville . . . remember my vision . . . he's got appendicitis!"

"I'll handle this!" he snapped, his Leo personality rising to the fore. "Tom, go and lie down!"

Nonplussed and anxious, I accompanied a doubled-over Tom to his bunk bed. As he climbed up, obviously in agony, he whimpered, "It really hurts." His eyes pleaded with me, his only hope.

"I know, sweetie," I said, momentarily cursing my position as stepmother and the unspoken agreement that I should always defer to their father for the major decisions in the children's lives. But this was urgent. Life or death. No time for demarcation lines and fragile egos. I had to make Neville understand. "I'll talk to your Dad again."

Returning to the kitchen, I tried again despite Neville's hostile behavior. I knew he would have died for his children. It was just one of the reasons I had fallen in love with him. But our relationship was still so new I sometimes didn't understand what made this man react so unpredictably. Why was he acting so strangely now? Wasn't he worried about his son? Or was it fear?

"Neville, if we don't take him now, it could burst," I urged. "Remember—"

Before I could mention the word "vision" again, he threw down the spoon, stomped past me, and called out, "Tom! Let's go!"

Relieved that at least I could get the boy to the hospital despite Neville's emotional reaction, I helped Tom down from the bunk and supported him as we shuffled out of the house and into the car.

The surgeon didn't have to poke very hard or very long to determine that Tom's appendix was, indeed, the problem. Thirty minutes after he was admitted, he was taken into the operating theatre to have the offending organ removed.

Later, as Tom's mother and I sat waiting for him to come out of surgery and Neville paced the shiny-floored hallways, she admitted, "I feel so bad. He was complaining of stomach pains all day, but I thought he had a bug and would be okay."

Strange, I thought, how both parents had ignored my warning and even now didn't acknowledge my precognition and the serious plight their son had been in. Maybe it would have challenged their belief systems to acknowledge that I had been able to accurately predict this event. Or was it their guilt about the breakdown of their marriage and the subsequent chaos their children were plunged into that made them want to deny the truth of this new drama and the emotional upheaval it might trigger? Perhaps it was a parent's fear of a child's being operated on? What did I know? I wasn't a parent, not a biological one anyway. And if I hadn't seen the image beforehand, would I too have waited too long?

As the surgeon wheeled Tom back into the ward, awake but still groggy from the anesthetic, the doctor stated, "Good thing you brought him in when you did. The appendix was just about to rupture, and he would have contracted peritonitis."

Afterward, Neville never mentioned my prediction. If he had said, "Thank you" or credited me with the vision in any way, it might have made my psychic gift real for him. Maybe he just wasn't ready for that. Later he did confess he had been scared at the prospect of his son "going under the knife." And he had had no time to emotionally prepare. Maybe seven-year-old Kyle summed up the family's version of the psychic episode most succinctly, "Creepy!"

I was just glad I had been there, and Tom was kept safe.

The protective white light really does work. Sometimes it works by showing us *the action* that needs to be taken in order to *manifest* the protection it offers.

14 How Does White Light Work?

Dear Natasha,

I often hear people say you can protect yourself or your loved ones with the white light. But how does it work?

Dear White-Light Seeker,

Some might say that the protection of the white light is the work of angelic presences. For the more pragmatic amongst us, this protective force is also explained as a matter of physics and/or faith.

The field of physics posits two likely scenarios for manifesting energy: energy attracts like energy (positive plus positive or negative plus negative) and complementary forces are attracted to one another (parts form a whole). Our thoughts are magnetic energy impulses, and so we will draw to ourselves the manifestation of those thoughts lying in our consciousness.

White light represents the lightest and most loving of vibrations, while the dark colors—gray to black—can represent manifestations of fear and evil. If you hold fearful thoughts in your mind and expect the worst, you are inviting negative experiences into your world. Just worrying that some awful thing might happen is enough of a negative experience, let alone actually manifesting a disaster! Fortunately, because the Universe's natural flow is creative—and not destructive—manifesting positive outcomes with thought is much easier than turning negative thinking into reality.

When we switch on a light in a darkened room, the darkness disappears. Light always overpowers darkness. Vibrating at completely opposite ends of the spectrum, light and dark are not normally attracted to each other—unless the dark is looking for a challenge! Because light is death to darkness, dark will usually avoid light at all costs. By choosing to encase ourselves in white light then, we are holding the intention to protect ourselves not only from potential harm but also from our neuroses about that potential harm.

As you surround yourself with the security of the white light, psychologically and energetically, your thoughts change from a lower vibration—fear and all things negative—to a much higher vibration—love and all things positive, including safety. When putting yourself in a bubble of white light—even if you are energetically unaware—your physical body language, your mental expectations, and your aura shift to emit a much more positive vibration of energy. So if like attracts like and you are emanating light, you will only draw to you that which is light and all things good.

What is also required to stay safe is undiluted faith in the white light. This light has *never* let me down, but then I've always had absolute faith in its power. I have always believed that it *would* protect me, and so it did. Faith or *knowing* in and of itself is what makes energy become manifest. (See Chapter 13: "I See! I Get The Picture!" in *Aaagh! I Think I'm Psychic (And You Can Be Too).)*

The white light is also handy-dandy for claiming parking spots, protecting your car from theft, and preventing accidents. I put white light around my vehicle when I drive a particularly hairy stretch of highway. Sometimes I add blue (creativity), green (harmony), and purple (spirituality) for fun and to add a thicker metaphysical barrier between my car and snowy ditches, precariously large buses on icy roads, and maniacal, cell-phone-talking drivers.

Some metaphysical teachers have disputed the necessity for the protective white light. The philosophy that "We don't need to protect ourselves as we should walk in faith" has been touted. I would wholeheartedly agree . . . if we were all highly evolved. However, as enlightened as I am by some people's standards, I also confess to being human . . . and I still experience fear. Sometimes I don't have faith in my own safety and I will ask for the white light to save me, if from nothing else, from the rantings of my own occasionally neurotic mind.

As you can see from the previous story, the white light also works around other people, particularly when we are not present physically to support them. And the white light is not restricted to physical protection. What if we can't reach a loved one who is suffering emotionally and engaging in self-destructive behavior?

We have all probably known a person with addictions or have been one ourselves. Negative subconscious beliefs take over our rational minds, and we will often sabotage our potential for happiness by actively destroying the good in our lives. While we are all on our own timetables for growth and healing—all of us "dancing as fast as we can"—and no one knows that timing but ourselves, we are not meant to stand by helplessly while the ones we love self-destruct, or even worse, die. Naturally, frustration, hurt, anger, and feelings of powerlessness will set in when we, the witnesses to that destruction, can't reach those loved ones—on the conscious level—to save them from themselves. The same applies if *we* are on the downward spiral and wondering how we can find the strength to pull out of the negative spin so we can return to a positive equilibrium. Feeling helpless and scared about the health of our family, our friends, or ourselves is not an empowered state. But it can be changed, and we *can* impact our loved ones, from a distance, with our love.

Here's how.

Instead of nagging the person into healing, I recommend that we telepathically wrap the self-destructive person in a cocoon of bright white light and envision them being well. If our intention is coming from unconditional love, then it will be received by the wounded person as love. Conversely, if our intention is coming out of a need to control or to make them better according to our agenda, the intention will fail. Imagining the wounded person being happy and well adds positive energy to their aura and is a protective shield that, if they accept it on the *unconscious* level, is supportive of their recovery. At the same time, if the wounded person really doesn't want your support, they will *unconsciously* reject the offer. After all, some people don't want to get well. Sometimes victimhood comes with payoffs. Some people just aren't ready to take responsibility for their lives while some enjoy their masochistically painful dramas and just want to be miserable—at least for a little longer.

However, if they do need psychic emotional support—which is most often the case—but they are too ashamed, proud, or humiliated to ask for help, the light of unconditional love works subtly on the alpha (unconscious) or subconscious levels where it can be more effective and where the ego state puts up less resistance.

If you are uncomfortable using the white light on another, you can, verbally or psychically, ask their permission. Enveloping a loved one in white light is, after all, the same as sending caring love. Who in this world doesn't want more love? Well, okay, some don't.

Should the rejecter of your love feel he/she doesn't deserve support, the worst thing that can happen is that your good wishes will just bounce off his/her aura like a boomerang and come right back to the source . . . you. The same dynamic would apply to a curse . . . but that's a whole other story.

So, **dear White-Light Seeker**, whether you choose to see angels, physics, or faith as the instrument of white-light protection for you and others, just *believing* in the power of the white light is what gives it its power.

RATS!

"You come runch."

I realized Lydia was addressing me. We were emerging together from the hall where we had attended a videoed talk by the Dalai Llama. I had met this Chinese woman on other occasions and was aware that, like me, she had a following of spiritual students, but our styles were totally different. A neighbor of this enigmatic woman who happened to be a friend of mine had often wondered at the slightly cultish feel of her following. She had commented that Lydia had a my-way-or-the-highway kind of practice, whereas I prefer to encourage my clients to find their own inner voices and follow them. Each of us chooses our way, time, and facilitator for healing. Whatever works! But my intuition had warned me to maintain a little distance from her. Now I wondered, was she issuing an invitation to lunch or making a demand?

"I have to get back to my writing . . . ," I muttered, hearing the lack of commitment in my own voice.

"Ach, liting!" she scoffed. "You come."

Well, I thought, *I so rarely interact with her, what harm could lunch do?*

"Okay," I said. It wouldn't be the first time I had chosen socializing over being a hermit. The next chapter of my book would have to wait.

Fifteen minutes later I was sitting at a table in the local Chinese restaurant with Lydia and five other women, members of her group. There I first laid eyes on Susan. I knew I would have something spiritual in common with her as she was one of Lydia's students, but what struck me so forcibly about this funky forty-five-year-old woman were her piercing blue eyes. Something else about her compelled me to pay attention, too. Anger. The effect of it was unmistakable, not just in her eyes but in her whole body.

When Lydia noticed that Susan and I had struck up a conversation, she said, "I tell her she come see you for a leading."

I could see just how much of a dominant force Lydia was in these women's lives. The chopsticks of all five women were poised in mid-air whenever she spoke, none of them wanting to miss any gems of wisdom that might fall from her lips. Was this kind of adulation healthy? My friend had reported watching from across the street in cynical wonder as a troupe of yuppie-like men and women marched into Lydia's house every Wednesday night. So even though Lydia had invited me to participate in the pre-session meditations of those weekly gatherings, my intuition had screamed at me to stay away. Maybe my friend was right.

"I would love to give you a reading," I responded directly to Susan, sensing that we needed to get to the root of that anger.

"Any chance of an appointment tomorrow?" she asked.

"Sure," I replied, mentally shoving yet another writing day aside.

The next day, as Susan sat down in my reading room, I was taken aback yet again by the ferocity in her eyes. *Wow! I wonder what or who she's angry with*?

It didn't take long for me to find out. As I took her hands and instantly felt her energy, a vivid picture flashed into my mind.

"Are you terrified of rats?" I asked, looking into her eyes to gauge her reaction.

She jolted as if I had just sent ten thousand volts through her body. Her eyes flashed daggers like thousands of tiny icicles.

"I *hate* rats," she hissed.

"I'm not sure if this experience is from this lifetime or a past life . . . but are you just *afraid* of rats or really *phobic*?" I enquired, already knowing the response.

"Probably phobic." Susan peered into her hands as if she would find the answer there.

"Do you have a memory of them in this life?"

"No."

I thought so. This trauma seemed like an old, old experience for Susan. I closed my eyes to go deeper into the feeling. What I saw made me shudder. "I feel like I'm hanging from a wall . . . . My wrists . . . . I'm shackled . . . ," I told her, as I lifted my arms up behind me as if I had been in that place, dangling from chained wrists. "They hurt . . . ,"

I continued. "My wrists hurt . . . . It's in a dark, dark place . . . like the dungeon in a castle . . . and I see rats, lots and lots of rats."

Once I gently took her hands in mine again, Susan's fear was evident as her nails dug into my palms. I opened my eyes and kept my tone of voice as matter-of-fact as possible in an attempt to ease her distress—and the pain in my palms. "I don't know if the rats actually bit you or you were just terrified that they would." I shuddered. "Does that make any sense to you?"

Even though we have no conscious memory of our past lives, my clients will have one of two reactions when I present them with a psychic image of their old experiences. They either gasp with vague recognition or stare blankly right back at me with a what-the-hell-are-you-talking-about look. Susan's reaction surprised me. Her eyes glistened with a fierce cognition.

"Ohmigod!" she exhaled. "There's something about that . . . ."

I closed my eyes again, attempting to dig deeper into her psyche, to enlarge upon the details, but a tremendous rage surged through me. "A huge injustice was done to you," I whispered, squeezing her hands in validation. Then suddenly the images faded. "I'm not getting any more. Maybe we should do a past-life regression?"

"I'd love to . . . ," Susan breathed, "but I'm leaving for home tomorrow. I live near Nanaimo."

"I'm coming to Nanaimo to do readings in three weeks. We could do it then."

Later that month I stood on Susan's doorstep, bracing myself for whatever we would both see. Neither of us would be prepared for what was to come.

As she lay on her daughter's single bed, I covered her with a blanket, explaining that the body temperature often drops during a regression. I had no idea how cold *I* would feel during her process.

To begin a regression, I take the client through a releasing and healing journey, bringing in the light of Divine Intelligence, angels, and guides so that the client is protected psychically and feels completely safe to relax into her own mind. Then if the client wants, she can use this light to clear any energy blocks, release tension, and soften any hurts—emotional or physical—before we begin the journey back into the past.

I suggested to Susan that she go back to the original lifetime and the source of her anger. When she was completely relaxed, I probed. "Where are you?"

In this relaxed state, the brain seems to take a lot longer to send messages to the mouth. But after a while, her lips moved and she whispered, "I'm in England . . . in a castle."

"Are you male or female?"

"Female," she uttered sleepily. "I'm the daughter of a lord."

"Can you tell me the date?" I asked. Sometimes being able to validate my client's story historically helps them trust their own feelings more.

"Twelve hundred something . . . not sure."

"That's okay. I want you to go to a significant event in that life . . . . After the count of three, find yourself witnessing the event. One . . . two . . . three . . . . Tell me what's happening."

Her eyes started to flicker as her mind searched her vast subconscious databank of memories.

"I'm . . . quarreling . . . with my father."

"What about?"

"About the man . . . his friend . . . . He's very angry."

"Why?"

"Because I wasn't supposed to be seeing him."

"Why not?"

"He wants me to marry his friend . . . and now I can't marry him."

I didn't understand this logic but I just let her mind lead where it wanted to go.

"Do you resolve this quarrel?" I asked.

"No . . ." Her voice dropped off and tears trickled down her cheeks. I knew we were getting closer, and I let her access her full memory.

"What's happening now?"

"The baby!" she said, her voice barely a whisper.

"Do you have a baby by this man?"

"Yes." The tears turned into crying sobs.

"Remember that everything you are seeing is just as a witness," I reminded her. "You are now completely safe in this time."

Her breathing, I noticed, was getting faster, a sign of anxiety. I reminded her once again that nothing could harm her and that she could slow down her breathing.

"I'm in the dungeon! . . . Ohmigod!"

I was surprised. Rarely when I pick up on a past life during a reading does the client recall that particular lifetime in a regression. Could this be the same trauma I had seen in her reading? "Tell me what you see."

"It's so dark . . . . I can hear . . . trickling water . . . and the rats!"

"From your safe place in this world, tell me about the rats."

"They're all around . . . everywhere," she sobbed in fear.

"Remember," I coached, "you're just watching what's happening. Are the rats hurting you?"

Susan moved on the bed as if trying to get out of her own body. "No . . . but they keep looking at me as if they want to."

"Why are you in the dungeon?"

"My father . . . punishment . . . for the baby . . . ."

"Where is the baby now?"

" . . . Dead." The coldness with which she said the word should have prepared me for what was to come.

"How did the baby die?"

The tears trickled once more down her pale cheeks, silent but steady. "My father . . . killed him."

Before I could prompt Susan with a "how," she volunteered the information. "He held my baby upside down by his leg and took his sword and cut him down the middle."

Oh, god! How cruel we humans can be to each other. The image of this brutality took my breath away, the revulsion thick in my throat. I had an urge to throw up, but I had to remain present and neutral for my client at this crucial point in her regression. As I studied Susan's face carefully, the enormity of her rage wasn't evident. Instead, it was in her long exhalation as if she herself had just realized how she felt about this murder.

"Keep breathing," I instructed, as I took a long, deep breath myself, "and tell me how you're feeling."

No sound. Just tears trickling silently down her cheeks.

"If you and I could go back to that time with your guides and angels and bring justice to the situation, what would you like to do?"

I could see that beneath her closed eyelids, her eyes were moving from side to side, searching, but no answer came.

"Why was your father so angry at you and your baby?"

"Because he wanted me to marry his friend. He was punishing me."

I'll say.

"It was for the sake of the country," she added, as if she understood or was rationalizing his behavior.

"Have you been reunited with the soul of that baby since that time?"

Susan's eyelids twitched as she searched her mind. "Yes!" She sounded surprised. A big smile suddenly lit up her face. "He's my youngest daughter in this life."

Now I realized we were going to be able to begin healing two issues in this one session, the rat phobia and the guilt. The tapestry of our soul journey has many loose threads until we tie them up.

"Would you like to ask your baby in that life for forgiveness?"

A small gasp escaped her lips as she realized that her rage was against herself as much as it was against her father, the rat.

"Yes," she breathed. The tears flowed freely now.

"Ask the baby now: Do you forgive me? And tell me what his answer is."

After a long pause, she said, "Yes . . . . He forgives me . . . . He says it was karma from another lifetime."

"Now are you able to forgive your father in that lifetime in England for what he did to you and your baby?"

She faltered while she searched inside herself. I expected her to say no. "Yes," she finally whispered huskily.

"Good. Now ask him if he would like your forgiveness."

Her nod was barely perceptible.

"Do you recognize that man as anyone in your current life?"

"My ex-husband!"

"Do you think that perhaps he was afraid of what would happen if you showed that illegitimate baby to the world?"

Another miniscule nod.

"Knowing that forgiveness is not being willing to carry the pain of what that person did to you any longer, are you willing to let your pain go?"

During the long hesitation that followed, I could feel her searching her soul for the compassion that she would need for herself and for him. Finally a long, "Yes-s-s-s-s" hissed from her mouth, as if all the air was being let out of an over-inflated tire.

Thank God. Her forgiveness would set her free, not only of her tie to that lifetime but of all the rage she had lived with for centuries. With the new ending to this tragic story, I had a sense that her whole world had rearranged itself into a new vibration of healing. While I knew that forgiving him and herself did not magically erase all the rage and anger in her soul for the last eight hundred-odd years, perhaps it had started the healing process in the present time. And the fact that she recognized both these characters in her movie, her father and her baby, was proof to me that we keep reincarnating with the same people until we learn the lessons, heal the rifts, and move forward together into higher vibrational lessons.

One thing I do know is that the lessons are eternal. For her, this healing was the beginning of a bigger awareness of who she was. There are no victims—though in the moment of the abuse we can be physically powerless.

After this session, I suggested to Susan that she take some time to assimilate this new information. Past-life regressions are often the gifts that keep on giving. Years after my own regressions, I have had many "ah-ha" moments where I have finally realized what the bigger lesson of that past experience was.

"Eventually, you may want to do another session and go deeper," I added. "Or you can just continue your work with Lydia. Whatever works."

Two weeks later Susan called. "The past-life session definitely brought up a lot of stuff for me, and I've decided to continue with Lydia," she informed me somewhat shyly.

"Good! I'm not surprised," I responded. "That regression was huge, Susan, and not just for you but also for the spirits of the other players in your movie. I'm just happy you have the awareness and the courage to keep addressing your issues and keep moving forward. That's all any of us can do. It's called growth."

15 Can a Past-Life Regression Help Me?

Dear Natasha,

I have a bird phobia. A friend told me that a past-life regression would help me get over my fear, but if I don't believe in reincarnation, how can it help me?

Dear Phobic,

The end result you want, I assume, is to be free of this fear so you can be the powerful person that you inherently are. The quick fix answer is to simply change your thoughts about birds from *birds will hurt me* to *birds are my friends*. But it's not that simple, is it?

Whether or not this fear originated in a past life or a childhood trauma, the result is the same. Conscious and subliminal fears can affect our psyches on a daily basis, but as with an infected tooth, when the pain starts to take over our lives, it is time to find the root cause and pull it out.

Sometimes phobias are triggered by suppressed traumas. For example, on the day the mother of one my clients died, my client saw a flock of crows sitting on her back fence. She was just five at the time. Years later her mind still associated crows with that pain. Whatever your story, you need to complete the trauma, a process that will require help.

While several modalities, such as NLP (Neuro-Linguistic Programming), EFT (Emotional Freedom Technique), and trauma counseling, will eradicate phobias, undergoing a past-life regression is also an effective healing method. Much can be achieved in one session. Believing in reincarnation is useful but not necessary. Let's assume for a moment that I am delusional and reincarnation doesn't exist: all we have is one earthly life. Nevertheless you choose to do a regression. Here's how it works.

Your subconscious mind is a humungous database that stores every experience you have ever had. In the process of a regression, you undergo guided visualization during which the alpha level of your mind, a semi-unconscious state, opens up a trap door to the subconscious. While you are still conscious of your present surroundings, you are also able to access all your past information from that database. When you ask your mind certain questions in this alpha state, the answers will surface from the subconscious. Be assured that the mind has its own amazing defense mechanism and won't show you anything you are not ready to see. The images that normally present themselves to my clients from their subconscious minds are always perfect for them at the time of the regression. I have never, for example, had anyone run screaming from the room or start foaming at the mouth on my couch despite the sometimes shocking dramas they were witnessing!

During the process of recall, I offer suggestions to the client about how the fearful associations—in your case, birds—or the memory of the trauma—can be changed to a more loving context. By exploring the experience and placing it in the context of a gift, your old wounds can heal, allowing you to return to your center of power.

After the deeper work is done, when you emerge from the alpha state and are fully back in your waking, ego-conscious level, you undergo a debriefing so you understand what your mind has just showed you. To receive the healing, therefore, it is not compulsory to believe in other lifetimes, just to believe in the now. Whether past lives are real or not, today you are the sum total of all your experiences. Being willing to deal with the now is the only focus you need in order to heal.

But does reincarnation exist? We all choose our own reality. For many people reincarnation is just a nice way of packaging a belief system. Some pooh-pooh the idea of recurring lifetimes, claiming it is just "an easy way out" so that if we don't complete our soul's work in this lifetime, we can say, "No worries, mate. I'll do it next time around." For me, having to come back to another life and do it all over again is a much scarier concept. As the Hindus say, "It's not death I fear but being born again."

Although I have done regressions that have helped heal many people, and encourage regressions, I continue to keep an open mind about the evolution of our souls. I choose not to believe *anything* because believing confines me to a limited box. With no walls around my thoughts, the theories are limitless. I can then continue to evolve instead of staying stuck in one tenet. My mantra is "Anything is possible."

Let us just for the moment suspend our disbelief in reincarnation. If my client is *not* remembering a past life during a regression, what *is* it then that he/she experiences—and I also see—when we delve into her soul? Where *do* those clips of movies come from that show up on both our psychic screens? Do we just have vivid imaginations? But then why do my clients gasp in recognition when I see their past-life experiences in a reading? Why do they respond with "Ohmigod! I've always felt that happened to me in another lifetime," or "Isn't that funny? I've always been attracted to that country"?

Of course, these pictures of past lives might be merely metaphors for our current experience. Just as in a dream, the mind will spew up a picture as an answer to our question. For example: Why am I afraid of green curtains? The mind knows on some level and will show us an image that we *think* is from a long-ago past, giving us some emotional distance and perhaps making us feel safer than a more recent horrific memory would.

In the preceding story my client was terrified of rats. The image we both saw—I saw them because she was holding them in her mind—could have been a metaphor for the feeling-guilty-and-needing-to-be-punished syndrome. Being shackled to a dungeon wall represented her powerlessness—her back to the wall—in her relationship with her father—God, patriarchal authority, or male archetype. Her father murdered her baby—her inner child, her innocence—for her disobedience—her expression of her individuality. The terror of rats represented the ugliness of her situation, her fear of death, and, on some level, her feeling that she deserved to be attacked.

Through my readings I understand that we are student gods and goddesses: we are in the process of raising our spiritual consciousness so we can become more godlike. As characters in our own unscripted movies, we are living out the roles we have chosen for this life without the advantage of dress rehearsals. As we fumble our way for the first time through the challenges of our existence, why are we so hard on ourselves? Would we berate a toddler who falls down when learning to walk? So why do we hold onto guilt—and seek punishment—when we are just students in this movie called life?

Our deepest fears arise from our fear of *punishment* that we *think* we deserve due to our perceived guilt around deeds past. A big part of our journey, therefore, is to free ourselves from that guilt, real or imagined. Once we are forgiven, the expected punishment and the fear of that punishment evaporate. By having compassion for ourselves and being able to forgive the self and others, we can set ourselves free and once again become the innocents we truly are. Life's lessons are always about compassion and loving the self more.

So, **dear Phobic**, before going through the deeper process of a past-life regression, you might first explore more surface causes. Birds, for example, may actually represent a fear of something else, such as flying. Flying = freedom = responsibility which can trigger feelings of inadequacy and of being overwhelmed. When we are overwhelmed, anxiety, panic, paralyzing fear, and finally depression are often right behind, and we can project these onto someone or something outside ourselves. For example, birds! All these emotions can then be triggered by the mere sight of birds!

In your case—and this is just an example—perhaps in a past life you were literally abandoned in a desert and suffered an agonizing demise by being pecked to death by a wake of vultures! No wonder you might feel a tad uncomfortable around birds! Identifying the source of the fear and bringing it to consciousness is the necessary first step toward breaking the hold the fear has over you.

The following methods can help rid you of fear:

- Find a trusted counselor with whom you can explore the fears that birds might represent in your life.
- Visit a hypnotherapist who is also open to the past-life theory and who can put you into a relaxed state to determine where the original fear came from and then guide you through the healing process.
- Visualize your life without this fear. Instead of thinking of birds as your feared enemy, think of them as your friends, your protectors, and messengers of happiness.
- Ask, in a meditation, what the birds-as-metaphor is teaching you. For example, are you afraid of your own power? Does freedom overwhelm you?
- Breathe deeply whenever you sense panic or feel fear or terror rising. Repeat your loving-bird thought.
- Know that this experience holds a gift for you within it. And you may have to work for the gift!
- Affirm that you are courageous, powerful, and in charge of your life.

When you are ready to see birds as emissaries of light, envision a single bird off in the distance. Gradually bring the bird closer until you have fully accepted the bird as your friend.

If you do decide that reincarnation is possible and that your bird phobia *might* have deeper roots in a past life, then you could explore a past-life regression. While you don't have to believe in reincarnation, it is important that you trust the practitioner, that you feel as safe as possible, and that you are open to being healed—whatever the process.

Whichever route you choose to help you overcome your phobia—counseling, visualization, or past-life regression—know that your fear, though real to you, *is* just a thought. In the meantime, here is an affirmation for you: *My loving thoughts are my protection. I am innocent and birds are my friends. In my world, I am always safe.*

Whether you are focused on your past, present, or future, doesn't that feel good?

DON'T DO IT!

"You're going to a concert in about two weeks," I told Sophia.

At first she frowned, then her huge brown eyes darted to the left, thinking. "Two weeks . . . ? Oh, yes. That's right!" She beamed. "We're all going to see the Grateful Dead at the Coliseum."

Sophia, a pretty twenty-something, had come to me for a reading in the resort town of Whistler. She had been one of my staff in my last job as manager in a local hospitality company. This reading wasn't her first with her ex-boss so she was already well aware that my accuracy rate was high. The European trip I had predicted for her a year earlier and the tall, young Norwegian she would fall in love with in Oslo had already materialized.

"I see a green mini-van and a young, blond-haired man driving," I said. "There are about six of you in the van."

Sophia's eyes were wide now. "How do you—?"

"But don't come back that night," I blurted. I shuddered envisioning the people in the van, all in their early twenties.

"Why not?" she asked.

"I don't know exactly." The dread in my stomach sat like a rock. "It could be a drunken driver, a landslide, an avalanche."

Highway 99 from Vancouver through Squamish to Whistler has long been notorious for being one of the most dangerous stretches of highway in North America. If they had placed crosses at the location of every accident and death, tourists might have been forgiven for mistaking them for a white picket fence stretching along the highway. I wouldn't have been surprised to see on that road the ghostly specters of all those people whose lives had suddenly been extinguished.

"Oh, everyone worries about that road." Sophia grimaced as if I were just echoing a parent.

"No, what I'm seeing is about *you* and your friends." Clasping her hands, I repeated, "Whatever you do, Sophia, please promise me you won't drive back that night. Stay in Vancouver."

"Okay!" She smiled nervously at my intensity.

"And don't let the blond-haired man drive."

"That's Tyler." She tilted her head as she always did when she wasn't clear on something. "How come?"

"He's not mature enough for all that precious cargo."

"Oh, yes," she said, nodding. "He *is* a bit wild."

In the previous few years, an unnaturally large number of young people from Squamish had died on that road. The majority of my staff of fifty young people lived there and had already attended too many funerals in their young lives. When my partner, Karl, had suddenly died of a heart attack the previous year, some of them had apologized for not coming to his service because, they said, "We just couldn't do another funeral." I understood. One was hard enough.

Three weeks later I bumped into Sophia in the village.

"Did you go to the concert?" I inquired.

"Yes, but we stayed overnight."

Thank the Lord. The potential danger had passed.

"And we didn't let Tyler drive."

Obviously.

"But Caroline drove her own car home," Sophia added, talking about her best friend, another of my former staff.

"And she's okay?"

"Oh, yes."

Phew.

I thought about what might have been. Maybe it was Tyler's driving that would have been the danger. Whatever it was, it was no longer a threat.

Sophia didn't have to listen to my advice. But perhaps she already knew on a subconscious level that danger was imminent. After all, when I read, I am tuning into the client's subconscious. Perhaps bothered by that niggling bad feeling, she had wanted confirmation, clarification, validation, or just a name for it. She had come to me so she could go back to her friends and say, "Natasha says . . . ."

Unlike Sophia, however, not all my clients are so responsive to the advice I give. Even after a stringent warning from yours truly, they either barge headlong into really bad situations with nasty outcomes or through apathy allow themselves to be sucked back into the same old destructive patterns while I sit helplessly by. Oh, well. What's a psychic to do? People will do what they will do even when they know it's unhealthy, even dangerous. Sometimes humans stubbornly persist in doing the same old life lessons over and over again until they get the message. It's called free will.

This incident wasn't the only time I witnessed how intuition, when listened to, can save lives. But the next time, it would be my own life that would be saved.

§

"What's up?" Georgia asked as I stood up and scrutinized the ocean.

It was Christmas Day. My girlfriend and I were, as we had envisioned, lying on Hollywood Beach in Florida. We had thought we were doing ourselves a favor by escaping the snow of Whistler where Georgia lived and the persistent drizzle of the Sunshine Coast where I had just bought a home. But the holiday wasn't *quite* what we had expected.

My fiancé, Karl, had died just 22 months earlier, so this year was my second Christmas without him. After surviving the exquisite misery of my first "holiday" season in grief and December grayness, I had sworn that this year I would avoid all those nauseatingly contented families with their Christmas shopping, their joyous caroling, and all the other painfully happy trappings of the season. Then in June, when Georgia and her boyfriend had a dramatic break-up, she and I had made a pact. No matter what happened—boyfriend or no boyfriend—we would not be in British Columbia in December. Instead, we would be lying on a beach, preferably where they had never even heard of Christmas. If we were going to be alone and miserable, we might as well choose a warmer clime in which to be alone and miserable.

Besides, the way my luck was going with romance in this lifetime, I didn't believe I would ever meet anyone and fall in love again. Georgia was equally cynical. So being of like mind and situation, we had conspired to do what we were good at: escape, go into denial, read lots of books, laze in the sun, and fake happiness.

In July, Georgia had called me at work. She was excited. "Okay, Natasha, I've got us a great deal for Christmas. You're gonna love it!"

As she worked in the sales department of a luxurious five-star hotel, I pricked up my ears. She had access to "great deals."

"Okay, are you ready?" She giggled gleefully. "This trip includes . . . ahem . . . four nights in Miami, two nights near Cape Canaveral, a cruise to the Bahamas, four days in the Bahamas—"

"Oooh," I heard myself say.

"No, wait, wait. There's more . . . and then . . . tickets to Disneyworld!"

I could live without that part.

"And it's only $500 dollars!" she added as if she had to sell me on it. "And that includes flights to and from all our hotels and the cruise!"

"Sound's great," I told her over the cacophony of phones ringing in the busy office where I worked part-time. The words "Bahamas" and "500" in one sentence made it so-o-o-o-o tempting. But there must be a catch . . . .

"You have to make up your mind in the next 30 seconds," Georgia prompted.

That's good, I thought, because that's all the time I had. The phones were persistent.

"I should really read up on it . . . ," I said somewhat feebly.

"Oh, just say yes." Georgia was giggling again, already anticipating the fun we would have.

"Er . . . er . . . ," I was thinking I should at least see a brochure.

"Come o-o-o-n," she urged. "Just do it."

It did sound good. Why not? "Okay." I caved in, caught up in her excitement, forgetting my intuition *and* my cardinal rule: *Never do anything Georgia suggests because it always gets you into trouble.*

Murphy being Murphy of course, between July and December everything changed. In November, Georgia and her boyfriend Sam got back together. In August, I had moved from Whistler and bought a new house. After two months, I had fallen in love with Neville and his three children.

But Georgia and I had made a pact. And we had already paid for the tickets. We had to go.

On December 20 as we stood at the car rental desk in Miami where they were threatening to give us a tiny but gleaming red bucket to drive away in, a car that screamed we-are-tourists-so-please-shoot-us, I left the complaining to Georgia. She was so good at it. Apparently, she too had neglected to read the fine print on this so-called vacation deal. This trip, I was realizing, had nothing to do with any five-star property, let alone the one she worked for. When we finally arrived at the potentially rat-infested, two-star hotel with its floating-scum swimming pool, tired as we were, Georgia refused to stay there. So after more tedious negotiations, we moved.

Now it was Christmas Day and thankfully I was at last lounging on a beach in the sunshine but missing my new family. I should have been home with them, I thought, opening presents around the Christmas tree, preparing dinner, getting fat on Quality Street and Turtles, my own baking and turkey.

"I'm restless," I told Georgia who was lying on her beach chair reading my *Time* magazine. Was she missing Sam, too, I wondered?

"Go for a swim," she suggested, pre-empting my thought.

"I'm going to," I responded.

"In the ocean?" she enquired.

I was still eyeing the calm blue sea. "No, I don't think so. In the pool."

"Ach, go in the ocean." She squinted up at me, her YSL sunglasses appearing very Jackie O and her thick, curly, reddish-blonde hair getting blonder by the minute. Two things Georgia never skimped on: hair product and sunglasses.

"Nah," I replied, my eyes still on the gentle blue waves. "There are sharks in there."

"No-o-o-o-o," she scoffed. "That was years ago. They've gone now. Go in the ocean, girl. Isn't that what we came here for?"

Not to get my legs bitten off, I thought. I admit I stood there for another millisecond and actually contemplated going in. Children and adults were playing in the water and at its edge. The surf was rolling in, small innocent waves. The calm, blue surface appeared to be safe enough. It was what lurked beneath that bothered me. And my inner voice was saying, *Don't do it!*

I remembered my cardinal rule then. *If I do the opposite of what Georgia says, I will survive.* The thought of death by shark—even the remotest possibility of death by shark—scared me. So why put myself in harm's way? I was attached to my body parts. I wanted to keep them.

"See you in a while," I told Georgia and turned to walk up the beach.

"Ah, ya big wuss," she muttered into my magazine.

"Heard that!" I called over my shoulder.

A giggle was her only response.

The pool was shorter than the Olympic size I was used to and not as pristinely clean. Too many children were splashing ferociously in the middle. Doing laps, I decided, would have me going against the flow. But I told myself, still resisting the idea of the ocean, that if I just persisted with my regular up and down, the other pool-occupiers might see I meant business and get out of my way.

After I had counted 40 laps, I decided that was enough smacked-in-the-face-chlorine-imbibing for one day. Hell, it was Christmas Day, the first time I had ever done *any* exercise, let alone in a pool.

Throwing my towel around my shoulders, I strolled back to find Georgia. Was it five o'clock yet? Neville and I had exchanged love letters for this day and agreed to read them at the same time.

As I arrived back on the beach, something felt different. People were running frenetically in all directions. I spotted a tall, skinny man in a red T-shirt driving along the water's edge on an ATV standing up in his seat, furiously shouting and waving at people in the water. In the opposite direction, young female lifeguards in red t-shirts were screaming at the swimmers, their words carried away on the strong breeze.

"What's going on?" I asked Georgia, still immersed in her article and seemingly oblivious to the heightened activity.

"Huh?" she glanced up and, feigning nonchalance, said, "Oh . . . there was a shark attack."

"*What?*"

"Yeah," she said blithely as if we hadn't discussed the possibility of *Jaws* and me having a close encounter less than an hour ago. "An 11-year-old boy was bitten in the back of his lower leg."

"How far out was he?"

"Oh, right there!" Georgia pointed to the exact spot where I had briefly contemplated entering the ocean.

I gulped. *My god! If I hadn't listened to my intuition . . . ?*

"Is he okay?" I asked. Silly question. Who is okay after being chomped on the leg by *Jaws*?

"Oh, yes," Georgia said. "They took him off in an ambulance but he looked fine."

Fine? I don't think so. But I certainly felt fine having followed my inner voice and not succumbed to the dare of my friend to swim in shark-infested waters.

As I lay back down on my beach chair to read my love letter, I said *thank you* to my inner voice, my God, my angels, and any other spirits for telling me, *Don't do it!*

16 Are We Ruled by Destiny or Free Will?

Dear Natasha,

Is our life predestined or do we have free will?

Dear Thinker,

Good question! After 30 years of delving into people's souls, predicting futures, and seeing the multitude of variables we all deal with, the short answer to your question is: both free will and destiny are at work. The more pertinent query might be: *How do destiny and free will work together?*

Let's explore.

If we believe that our life paths are written in stone and we can do nothing about them except surrender to destiny, would such a belief not destroy our motivation to learn and grow? Such predestination implies we are powerless.

Or should we believe in blind luck—good or bad—random choices by some nameless higher power to bestow on us curses or blessings? Such randomness also implies that we are at the whim of the gods, still powerless.

But what if our thoughts created our positive or negative outcomes, good or bad luck?

I believe that while we have scripted parameters for our life journeys, our paths are not set in absolute granite. Free will also applies. The Universe is not chaotic but is ruled by laws of cause and effect, action and reaction, and other laws of energy, including the magnetism of our own conscious thinking.

Our scripted parameters offer us a theme for learning. Depending on our agreement before we came here, the theme will attract to us the people and events we need in order to learn its lessons. Mastering right use of power, overcoming fear, and surrendering to unconditional love are underlying themes for all of us.

As a psychic reader, I am privy to my clients' individual life themes. Before we begin our physical existence, while we are still in spirit, something similar to a flight plan of our imminent life is filed in the Akashic Records, what many believe to be the record of all our souls' lives. Based on our soul's progression through many lifetimes, this "flight plan" subjects us to a karmic destiny that can teach us what we need to learn or relearn—our required evolution. This flight plan is imprinted into our souls, spirits, and subconscious minds, but once we are physically born, the details of the plan are not readily available to us on the conscious level.

If we choose to fulfill the preordained destiny, we are then employing our free will. Conversely, if we *avoid* that destiny, we are still using our free will, although not for our highest good. The universe will not force us to grow. Whatever we resist persists, however, and so our lives will become increasingly difficult until we hear the message and surrender to the growth that is our destiny.

Even though the events from our flight plan are magnetically drawn into our lives, we also employ free will in choosing the thoughts we have *about* those events. These thoughts—positive or negative—not only alter the perception and therefore the experience of the event but can also change the outcome in the physical world. Our perception then becomes our reality. As Gregg Braden, author of *Walking Between the Worlds*, points out, an experience does not exist until our minds give it attention, and *what we focus on expands.* So, perception is a choice we make using our free will.

The old adage *Seeing is believing* has it backwards. We need to *believe* before we can *see.* The skeptic, the person who refuses to be open to anything invisible, will never be able to see good unless he or she is first willing to believe that good exists. Our thoughts are still ours for the choosing.

According to the manner in which energy syncretizes itself through the laws of attraction, we draw to us what we *perceive* as true in our world, whether it is true or not. Be warned: *The Universe always makes us right about what we believe.* For example, if I choose to believe the world is full of grumpy people, guess who I attract? Then I can say smugly, "You see, I'm right!" But it may be only *my* world that is full of grumpy people.

Negative events can often feel like punishments, and sadly, many people take setbacks personally. People who believe I-only-have-bad-things-happen-to-me simply perpetuate the attraction of negativity to themselves. Many of us are indeed subject to struggle patterns in which similar negative dramas keep recurring: fires, car accidents, failed relationships, illnesses, etc. Such repetitions can be mistaken for bad luck, bad karma, curses, or destiny. These lower vibrational patterns are usually set up in childhood, by past traumas, or in past lives. Some of us spend our time on this planet working through those childhood/trauma/past-life patterns until finally, at whatever age, when we are healed, we can be free. This process often involves being willing to meet and fight inner demons. Some people find the strength do this and win their lives back, while others are too scared to face and forgive their own dark side. Unfortunately, those people will never live out their greater destiny . . . not in this lifetime anyway.

Let's take a spirit, for example, whose specific destiny is to learn to forgive, overcome fear, and use his talent as an artist to communicate love and healing to the world. In order to be a great artist he needs to understand the human condition. He might undergo a traumatic event in his childhood that has the potential to sensitize him to the suffering of humanity. As a test of his free will, he has at least two choices for an outcome.

He can remain victimized by that childhood event. As he grows to adulthood, he presents as fearful, hurt, and small. He still paints but probably struggles as a starving artist. To sedate his pain, he might become an alcoholic and never influence the world with his work. Or . . . he could choose to see that early trauma as the teaching that gave birth to his artistic talent and forgive. He determines to dedicate himself to a higher purpose. He is motivated to help others understand their own painful pasts, and through his painting and in the healing of others, he heals himself. But first he would need the courage to rise above the frightened child and move into his greatness.

So what was his greater destiny in this lifetime? To love himself and to serve others.

Where could he use his free will? To be small or to become great.

But if honing the greatness of our souls is our higher destiny, why do we need to experience so much pain, physical and emotional? Perhaps painful challenges are the Universe's way of guiding us back onto the right path. If we are not listening to our truth, a metaphorical whack over the head is a sure sign from the Universe that we need to correct our stinking thinking. As Mike Conor, ISYS (I Speak You Speak) Radio Network interviewer and consciousness coach, once commented, "If I don't listen to my guidance, first it's a whisper, then a two-by-four, and then a train wreck."

Our intense pain and anger come from a deep soul-level recognition that we are not loving and honoring *ourselves* enough. Something needs to change. But pain is not the end result, just the messenger. Pain's job is to motivate us to listen to our spirits and help us realign with our intended flight path. How, when, and with whom we go through painful experiences and how long we stay in the pain is up to us. Therein lies the free will. We can see the pain itself as karma or we can ask the question: What is this pain showing me? Where do I need to adjust my compass?

With enlightened thinking and more light in our beings, perhaps we won't need to visit pain. According to Gregg Braden, reality as we currently understand it is shifting. Because of an increase in the vibrational frequency on the planet and within our own bodies, he asserts, we are rising above the heavy dense matter in which we have been existing. In my own visions, I was shown how those who are open and ready to accept the higher consciousness would become more light-filled. Like a 60-watt light bulb exchanged for a 200-watt bulb, our auras will be shining ever more brightly. Perhaps then we will be like the angels and take ourselves far more lightly!

Some people might appear confined by their destiny while others seem to be more free-spirited. Happiness and success seem to flow toward them. Does this mean that these spirits have more free will? Or are these "lucky" people just blessed with good karma? Is something else at work?

Maybe positive thinking is creating their success. While it may appear that they have more freedom, perhaps they simply choose to think more freely. Perhaps these positive thinkers simply *expect* success. Even when successful people meet obstacles, they tend not to judge the experience as good or bad or take the setback personally but accept the challenge as part of life, resolve the problem, and carry on. They don't allow adversity to stop them, and consequently their lives stay in the flow. The positive thinker acknowledges that each challenge or lesson has an inherent gift. "Disappointments" become simply a gift of universal guidance by raising the questions "What was I supposed to learn from that?" and "How can I do better next time?" Choosing to accept what is and then loving what is frees the spirit.

If you want to take your destiny into your own hands using free will, the following are some tips for beginning the process:

- Be aware of your own thoughts. Recognize the two sources of fearful thoughts: ego and intuition. When you are in the ego level, that small part of the mind will try to suck you into fear. That is part of the ego's job. Ego-constructed fear thoughts try to keep you small, and they usually reside in the head. Just ask your own mind, "Is this the truth, or is my mind making this up?" If you feel the fear thoughts are ego-based, repeat, "Cancel, Cancel. Love, Love." Then allow your mind to envision a more constructive outcome. On the other hand, with intuition-based fear you will usually sense dread in your gut and/or other parts of your body. Heed your intuition. Listen to the inner warning and take the appropriate action.

- Commit to a positive outcome, no matter how hopeless it looks.
- Decide that you deserve and can have it all if what you desire is for the higher good.
- Listen to your self-talk. Be your own coach.
- Affirm always what you want, not what you don't want.
- Assess how you are doing by the results in your life. Keep aligning with the greater you.
- Keep your mind on the destination. Visualize daily the destiny you choose.

Fulfilling our destiny constitutes neither a success nor a failure, just growth at our individual rates. Whether you fly low or high, you will get there eventually. As in any test, our efforts are also measured by degrees. We are in a school of sorts, and if we don't get straight A's, it doesn't mean we have failed. Only our guides, our God, and our own souls know the spirit's full capability for this lifetime. At the end of the life, our own souls will be the reviewer of our spirit and its flight, whether it strayed, delayed, or stayed on course.

So, **dear Thinker**, if you develop these positive habits, you will begin to see how you can use your free will to *fulfill* your greatest destiny. Freedom to fly higher *is* your destiny. Compassion, faith, and courage in every moment will empower you to rise above the darkness and fly as high as you want. Then you can become the amazing human being you are designed to be. But hey, it's your destiny, your free will, and your choice.

When you do choose greatness, some people just might mistake you for being ever so lucky!

17 ASSISTED SUICIDE?

"Sonya's really upset," my friend Becky announced on one of my regular visits to White Rock.

"How come?" I knew Sonya as Becky's tall, willowy, sensitive friend. I also knew she was a mental health worker who, like me, sometimes found other people's traumas too overwhelming for her own soul.

"One of her patients committed suicide last week."

"Oh, no!" Having any of my clients take his or her own life—when I hadn't been available to support them in their hour of need, or worse still, if I *had been* available and had said the wrong thing—was one of my worst fears. "Poor Sonya."

"Yeah," Becky added. "This girl had also become a friend." Getting emotionally involved with clients is probably against the rules in the government-run, red-taped, clinical world of mental health professionals, but avoiding personal involvement is easier said than done. The line between my own clients and my friends is often so smudged as to be non-existent. Fortunately, because I make my own rules and set my own boundaries around my work, the client/friend relationship still works for me. I remain—most of the time—within my professional lines.

"The suicide was quite messy," Becky continued.

"In what way?"

"Apparently she killed herself in her own apartment, but after she tried to slit her wrists and that didn't work, she hanged herself."

I groaned, imagining the grisly scene.

"Sonya wants to talk to you about it," Becky said.

"Sure," I said, "I'll talk to her." But I was already experiencing a sense of dread around this case.

A week later at the grand opening of Becky's new art gallery, I saw Sonya myself. Her porcelain skin was even paler than usual and her tall frame was stooped as if she were trying to curl up inside herself.

"Becky told me about your client," I offered, saving her the pain of repeating the story. "I'm so sorry."

Sonya's long, straight, brown hair fell around her face as she stared down into her drink. Even though suicide can be a decision made on a soul level and not merely circumstantial, the feeling of failure for those around the person who commits suicide is still devastating. "Yeah . . . thanks," she said.

"Is there anything I can do?" I asked.

"Actually . . . there is." Sonya and I moved to the corner of the gallery where we found two empty chairs and sat down.

"She's still there," Sonya said, staring intently into my eyes while lowering her voice, as if somebody might hear her already soft tones. I leaned in so I could hear.

"Where?"

"In her apartment. The new tenant keeps seeing her walking out of the bathroom and into the laundry room."

I shuddered as I picked up the energy of her dead client. It wasn't the image of the girl still haunting her old apartment that was most disturbing; it was the thick, dense darkness that surrounded her while she was making sure she would die.

"Do you think you can help?" Sonya asked.

"Yes, I'm pretty sure I can." But even as I spoke the words, my whole body clenched. As psychics go, I'm probably a bit of a chicken. I have never offered, for example, to work with the police on finding missing children. Finding adults who have disappeared is traumatic enough for me. I like to rationalize that looking for missing little people is just not the Universe's intention for me or the way I am meant to use my psychic gift. Or maybe . . . I am just a coward. "When do you want me to do it?" I gulped as I asked the question.

"How about the next time you're in White Rock?" Sonya suggested and downed the rest of her drink.

"That's about two weeks away," I offered, mentally checking my schedule. "Will that work for you?"

"Sure." As she stood up, she put her hand on my arm, the touch as fleetingly gentle as a butterfly landing on a flower. "Thank you, Natasha."

"There are no guarantees," I reminded her as she headed back into the crowd. When I said those words, maybe I already had a sense of what was to come.

Over the next couple of weeks I could not stop thinking about this poor woman who had been so desperate to die. I didn't even know her name, but her sadness haunted me. Maybe it was because my own mother, along with daily threats of putting her head into the gas oven, had attempted to kill herself by overdosing and hacking at her wrists with a blunt knife. But this woman had actually done the deed, persevering until it worked. Her actions were so brutal, so filled with dark desperation to be rid of her body and her pain that I became determined to help her find some peace.

But that changed a few nights before I was due to go to White Rock again.

The house is big and old inside. I am walking up the broad wooden staircase. Three people are standing outside the open door of her apartment, talking amongst themselves in hushed tones about what has happened inside.

I am almost at the apartment door when I am suddenly picked up by some invisible force. This energy—or is it several spirits?—holds me up, horizontally suspending me in the air, and spins me around and around, faster and faster. I panic. I just want the spinning to stop, to put my feet on the ground, to grab hold of something, but I can't. Aaagh!

Then I was jolted awake. With relief I realized I was in my own darkened bedroom lying in my own bed. The sound of my partner softly snoring beside me was a great comfort. I was tempted to wake him and tell him about my nightmare. But I knew it wasn't a bad dream. It was a psychic attack. The spinning wasn't a new experience for me, and the message I got from the spirits was loud and clear. *Stay away from the dead woman.*

Neville stirred beside me. "You okay?" he muttered sleepily.

"I just had a . . . nightmare," I told him, knowing he wouldn't want details at three in the morning.

He put his arm around me, pulling me close. As I lay in the comfort of his physical warmth, I decided, *That's it! I'll tell Sonya it's too much for me, and I'll find someone else, someone more equipped to deal with that kind of trauma.*

Then a few days later, after I had given Sonya the number of a spiritualist church to contact, something occurred to me that perhaps explained why I hadn't been able to get close to the dead woman's spirit:

the darkness around her repelled my lighter vibration. Perhaps those dark entities had goaded her to take her own life and were still holding her spirit hostage in some dark place. My psychic attack was, I knew, the dark entities warning me to stay away. It made sense that they did not want me to rescue her because I am of the light, and light is death to the dark. If I had been able to access her spirit after her death and bring her back into the light, those evil entities would have been down one recruit.

I also realized my own fears had created a portal through which the dark entities were magnetized to my lowered vibration—dark attracts dark.

I chose to pray for her soul, sending her my light remotely. On her soul level, I envisioned light penetrating her darkness and healing her disturbed spirit.

Two weeks later when I checked in with Sonya, she told me the incident had affected her so badly that she had decided to change careers. She also added that without any help from the spiritualist community, the sightings of the girl had stopped and the energy in the apartment lightened. I comforted myself with the thought that my prayers had worked. Perhaps, as I had requested, her angels had come to take her home where she would find love . . . and especially peace. I hoped so.

17 What Happens to the Soul of a Suicide?

Dear Natasha,

My friend recently committed suicide. I really miss him. What possesses a person to kill themselves and what happens to their soul?

Dear Bewildered,

First of all, I am sorry for your terrible loss and I pray that your feelings of grief, anger, confusion, helplessness, and disbelief are not compounded by other people's well-meaning but damaging opinions about suicide. As I state in my first book, I believe that many of us when we die have in some way given up our will to live—sometimes through apathy and sometimes with conscious or unconscious intention. Suicide takes many forms, and we don't have the right to judge those who are obviously in terrible physical and emotional pain. Committing suicide was a more drastic action for your friend than mere apathy and perhaps the only course he could see at the time to escape his personal hell.

One famous psychic states that suicides keep walking through a revolving gray door until they wake up to a higher reality. In the thirty years of my work in the psychic realm, I have encountered many spirits who have ended their lives, but I have never seen that revolving gray door! Not that one of us is right and the other wrong—all psychics see through their own perceptions, and all our visuals are open to interpretation. So if you are seeking out psychics to give you answers, be prepared for a variety of responses. You will have to decide which ones feel right to you. Be discerning with the information you receive—including mine! The following information is based on only my experience and perceptions.

What happens to us after we die, no matter how we die, depends on our willingness to accept the unconditional love and light that awaits us. While some suicides resist this light because of their own guilt, depressed consciousness, or regret, others are relieved and happy to have shed their physical bodies and their lives on the physical plane and to embrace the light. Consciousness is our mind/spirit and is just thought. So if we choose to think there is a hell and that we deserve to go there, guess what we experience? Conversely, if we believe in heaven and are willing to live in paradise, our minds will be open to that experience. The Universe (God, Creator) is all-loving. We, however, are much harder on ourselves.

Life is challenging for all of us. Sometimes the earth plane can be just too painful for some spirits to stay here, especially those prone to depression. People who take their own lives are in so much anguish, no matter how much they are loved, that they feel choice is just a word. At that final moment in their lives, death is the only antidote to their private hell. Through my psychic readings, I have gleaned that committing suicide has nothing to do with cowardice. The decision is not made lightly or without a lot of premeditation. And there are no accidents. The pain experienced before arriving at that final decision is intense. Once the decision is made, however, the person might demonstrate a euphoric happiness because they *have* finally made the decision. That final elation just prior to the suicide fools many of their friends and family into thinking that the depressed person is getting better.

Many psychics teach that suicides have to come back to complete the unfinished business of their lives, but we *all* reincarnate to repeat the lessons we don't learn—until we evolve. We can only move onto that higher and more joyous dimension when we have let go of those lower vibrations and earned a place in that higher realm. And while this physical life is a school, so is the spirit realm. Thus whether we are in the physical or in spirit life, the learning never ceases. In the scientific world of physics, according to the universal law of like attracts like, we would first have to be like the angels to be able to hang out with them.

Before anyone judges any soul who chooses to end his or her life, he would be wise to remember we may all have done the same thing in a past life. Smoking, extreme overeating, or taking drugs are often signs of suicidal tendencies, an unconscious intention to destroy the physical body. Suicide is just a giving-up of the will to live. When we die, we have all given up our will to some extent.

I have always been shown that once we are in the spirit realm, rather than being judged by the almighty, we judge ourselves, with a little help from our spirit guides. Our own souls rate us as to how we have performed according to our inherent greatness. Our soul essences then mete out what "attitude adjustments" or repeat lessons are required.

Some psychics purport that by committing suicide, the person has reneged on their soul agreement. But maybe committing suicide *is* the soul agreement, the drama through which they and those affected are to learn.

Each of our lives is a playing out of our soul's lessons. Imagine your life as a movie. A major character in your movie commits suicide. The learning inherent in this event is a part of *your* soul's agreement for this life. The fulfillment of this role motivates *you*, the family, and all the other people whom the suicide affects to wake up to a higher consciousness.

The suicide's soul agreement is similar to that of a child who dies young through accidental death. The child has a soul agreement in place, an agreement the child made with the family before he or she was born. Under the terms of the agreement, the child sacrifices a longer life so that the other people—parents, siblings, and friends—can wake up to a larger reality through their pain . . . if they so choose.

If suicide is part of an agreement, it can (but does not necessarily) show up in the hand, specifically in the head-line. This major line in the palm originates between the thumb and forefinger and crosses the middle of the hand from side to side, or slopes down toward the wrist. But when the head-line starts above the thumb, continues in a straight line for two or three inches, and then descends in a sharp vertical fall toward the wrist, the indication is that the person is vulnerable. But I want to state clearly here that having such a line *does not mean a person is destined to commit suicide*. However, they *could* be prone to depression and they need to do everything in their power to manage that aspect of themselves *in order to avoid* suicidal tendencies. While there are different types of depression, the usual antidotes to depression include exercising regularly, eating healthily, avoiding addictive substances, especially sugar, and associating with balanced, naturally upbeat, caring, grounded people. Perhaps the most powerful therapy for depression is expressing feelings through writing, art, conversation, or other creative expressions. Ever notice how many people with bipolar disorder, which is characterized by both depressive and manic phases, are brilliant artists?

Another type of depression, situational or acute depression, which is usually motivated by a set of negative circumstances, can also be aggravated by the suppression of unexpressed rage or a sense of powerlessness. This depression usually lasts until the person resolves his or her feelings about the situation. Sometimes this form of sadness can be alleviated by simply telling the truth about it. Don't get sad, get mad. But please . . . express that anger to a professional or to the person it concerns, and in a constructive way!

While some depressions may require ongoing care, in my world anti-depressants and shock treatment are a last resort. But if severe depression—whatever the cause—is not treated, suicide can be the outcome of that particular hell.

As in the previous story, the other danger of depression, especially if the person is both highly sensitive and psychically unaware, is their susceptibility to what I call low-life attachments. These are the lower-vibrational, dark, or even evil spirits of some deceased. They attach themselves to the vulnerable psyches of people who are still living and who are in a state of low vibration themselves, especially from depression, victimization, and/or anger. These nasty spirits fill the minds of the living with negative words and thoughts, urging them to do damage to others and/or themselves, including killing the self. What I am describing is a form of possession.

The living person is probably unaware they are psychically open to these negative energies. Believing that the destructive thoughts are, indeed, their own, they suffer even more self-hatred. Why do these low-life spirits haunt the vulnerable? Because they can. It is their only form of power in an otherwise powerless state. What do they want? More recruits. Misery loves company!

So, **dear Bewildered,** I am sure you must be going through all the "what if?" questions and wondering whether you could perhaps have done something differently to change your friend's mind and prevent what you perceive to be this tragic outcome. Know that none of us has the power to change another's life. As survival is the most powerful instinct within us, we are all capable of making the right choice for ourselves. So know that your friend did what he needed to do. In that way—harsh as this sounds—he *did* take care of himself the only way he knew how.

So whether depression, possession, or his soul agreement motivated your friend to take his own life, he is now where he wants to be. When your first stages of grief and anger have passed, think on the gift that he was to you while he was here. Ask yourself what his leaving in this way teaches you about your own life? Whatever your answer to this question is today or in the years to come, *that* is another of his gifts to you.

The gift *you* can give to *him* right now is to pray for his spirit to step into the light of unconditional love so he can return home to heaven and peace. From that place, he is eternally with you and can probably give you more love and friendship than he sometimes could when he was here on earth.

LIFE OR DEATH?

To: natasha@natashapsychic.com
From: SandyHope@changedthename.ca
Date: March 2, 2007
Subject: Am I going to live or die?

Natasha, I'm really ill. Can you give me a reading and tell me whether I'm going to live or die?

The e-mail from my long-time friend Sandy who lives in Nova Scotia jarred me out of my early morning, pre-coffee daze. If my father hadn't been on the brink of dying 10,000 miles away in Wales and my friend Angela hadn't been suddenly stricken with breast cancer and my artist friend hadn't been taken into hospital with a galloping heartbeat, maybe I would have reacted more mildly to Sandy's question. But I was beginning to feel overwhelmed by thoughts of death, dying, and other disappointments. Instead of getting sad, I was getting mad. I resented feeling powerless while friends and family were dropping like flies, so I chose to channel my anger into action.

Sandy was suffering from a tough and rare auto-immune disorder called myasthenia gravis. She has to take drugs every four hours just to keep her muscles, including her heart, functioning. As if that weren't enough, she was also fighting a cold. Maybe it had progressed to something worse, like pneumonia.

Forget e-mail, I thought. I picked up the phone and called her. Her normally strong voice sounded faint and wheezy as if she were struggling for breath. Her vulnerability was unnerving. I was more accustomed to, and in awe of, her ironclad resilience to life's challenges. In her career as a sales executive, she was known for her unwavering determination to overcome the relentless stream of obstacles thrown in her path. Usually, she would rant and rave for a day and then set about methodically resolving each problem. Her gargantuan efforts were eventually rewarded, and her reputation as a force to be reckoned with in her own field was now legendary. Her challenges would have thrown even me, Ms. Strong and Independent, into a state of overwhelming despair. So I had great respect for Sandy's fortitude, especially in the business world.

Although she was chicly feminine in her dress and physical presentation, her male aspect was more evident in her action-oriented behavior. I had witnessed first-hand how she and her team had sold a project in record time. She was the only woman in the group, "just one of the guys," she had said. *If you can't make 'em love you, join 'em* was probably embedded in her psyche.

Sandy had her softer side, of course—like a huge kind heart and a great sense of humor, particularly about herself. But she was often so blunt, especially about men, that I told her she scared me. And I was her friend; just what was she like with her clients? For years I had been warning her to forgive the men in her life or her negative thinking would have a destructive effect on her physiology and she would get sick. As a former microbiologist, she understood this concept, intellectually at least. But her grudging responses had always told me she wasn't ready emotionally to let the bastards off the hook. Or that's how she saw it. Then, sadly, ten years ago she had indeed contracted the auto-immune disorder.

"In answer to your question, Sandy, I am going to ask you this: do you want to live or do you want to die?"

Silence.

"It's not the biology that keeps us here," I added. "It's our will. Whatever you choose, I will support you. But *you* tell me what *you* want."

"Well . . . I want to live," she answered feebly.

"Do you . . . ?" At times Sandy had been so fed up with her illness and the havoc it wreaked in her life that I had worried she might succumb to its grip.

"At what age do you want to die?"

"I don't know," she scoffed.

"Yes, you do. Give me an age."

"Well . . . 82."

"That sounds good. Another 20 years then. Better be in good shape if you're going to live that long."

"Humph."

"Make up your mind. It's your life. *We* want you to stick around," I said, referring to our close group of nutty friends. In an attempt to edge her toward a decision, I said, "You could live for your children and your grandchildren but it's *you* you have to live for." Then I added, "I also get the sense that you're not done yet."

"Whaddya mean?" she probed, sounding like the Nova Scotia country yokel that we often teased her about being.

"I think you're meant to experience love, real love, romantic love—you know, the kind you studiously and stubbornly avoid. It's what we're most afraid of in this life that we're meant to overcome, and you haven't even come close to real love yet." I knew perhaps I was being a little rough, but I was pulling out all the stops for my friend. This conversation might be the only chance I had. No point in going soft now. "I still see that man I predicted. Remember? The ex-professor who's traveling at the moment? I see you laughing a lot together."

"Yes . . ." she said.

"Yes what?"

"Yes, I want to live." She exhaled the words, but her tone sounded definite, genuine, and it held a trace of her old flinty determination.

"Okay," I breathed, mentally rolling up my sleeves. "So we have some work to do. You need to do that forgiveness."

I heard another grunt, but it was a grunt of resignation. She couldn't avoid it any longer. Years ago I had purchased a large stack of beautiful, green bond writing paper and a big, fat, sage-smelling green candle. "Write to everyone you need to forgive and from whom you need forgiveness," I had said. "Either send the letters or burn them. If you burn them, ask your angels or your God to transmute that old pain into something beautiful, like blessings, love, or health, all sprinkled with fairy dust."

"Yeah, yeah," she had responded then, her dismissive words accompanied by an almost imperceptible snort.

And now the issue had raised its ugly head again, and it wouldn't be silenced until it was healed. As when we carry a low-grade virus, carrying old hurts only drains our energy. Some people, including me, really can't help being idiots sometimes. Sadly, many of us stubbornly hold on to the pain of hurting someone else or being hurt by them. We cling to our self-righteous justification or our righteous indignation, choosing to be right rather than happy. The only way I know to release those hurts is through a willingness to accept the spiritual lesson of the event. Once we can feel compassion for the perpetrators and ourselves—whether we are perpetrator or "victim"—and stop justifying holding onto the pain, we can move forward into a new, free, exciting world.

"The body will do what the mind tells it to, Sandy," I continued. "So talk to your body and give it permission to regenerate in a healthy way. Energy is always moving, always creating or destroying."

For the next ten days I called Sandy every day and coached her for an hour at a time, sometimes longer, using a combination of tools—Neuro-Linguistic Programming (NLP), visualization, affirmations, and a lot of humor. Gradually she began to sound more solid in her conviction that she could actually fight back and win this battle over the pneumonia that was weakening her already tired muscles.

On the weekend she called me. "Natasha," she panted, this time from excitement. "I had a dream!" she exclaimed, sounding like Martin Luther King. "I had a dream! I finally get what you've been telling me all these years."

I wasn't sure what she meant but I said to myself, *Finally. Hallelujah! Praise the Lord.*

"I realize I've just been giving lip service to my belief in God. I'm gonna forgive now. I'm just going to let it go. And I'm going to ask God to heal me."

"Well, Sandy," I interrupted, "that might work for some people, but not for you."

I heard a sharp intake of wheezy breath. These were not the words she was expecting to come out of *my* mouth.

"Why not?"

"Because you believe that God is male, a patriarch. And you don't trust men."

She emitted a miniscule harrumph as she got my meaning. "Then . . . how?"

"You *tell* God that He's *got* to heal you."

I heard my friend laugh.

Usually I promote the idea of co-creation with a higher power, but I knew Sandy needed to have not-an-ounce-of-doubt faith in her cells. It was paramount that she believe she had total power in this situation. For her, complete and utter conviction would be the only way it would work. Apparently we have more than 260 million cells in our bodies, and for healing to work, a person must have absolute faith in each one of those cells. To *ask* for healing meant a possible no-you-can't-have-it response.

By putting Sandy in the driver's seat in her own mind, her belief quotient or faith could then be absolute.

This woman, who could scare the pants off some big-time wheeler-dealers, now sounded vulnerable and confused. "Well, when I'm better, I'll give back somehow," she added, still having the desire to control.

"You can if you want to but you don't have to," I continued, confusing her even further. "Think about it. You say you hate men, yet you have virtually become one by adopting male energy. No wonder you have a disease that's eating you up inside. It makes sense to me why this is happening to you. To heal, you need to acknowledge and celebrate the feminine, allow yourself to be loved, allow yourself to receive, even from the big guy in the sky."

Sandy's weak but heartfelt chuckle signaled her understanding and, perhaps, her willingness to surrender.

"Sandy, you need to let your feminine energy just bre-e-e-athe," I said, exhaling a long breath myself. She was so tough. "Just receive the healing. Then maybe later you can give back. But just the miracle of your healing will be the gift to your God."

"Ohmigod, Natasha. That's bang on!" she exclaimed. "I'll do that," she added, even more resolve in her voice.

"You need to treat your healing just like you approach a sales deal." Now I was speaking her language. "I've watched you. You just decide it's going to happen and no matter what obstacles appear—great or small—you're like a Samurai. You just keep going until it's done. Do the same thing now with your vision of being healthy. Let's imagine you doing somersaults in your garden this summer when I come to visit you. Nothing else is an option."

Later that week I received a telephone call from David, Sandy's son. He sounded uncharacteristically scared. "Just letting you know, Mum's in the hospital," he said, struggling to keep his voice even. "It's not good. That pneumonia really weakened her system. We'll keep you posted."

For a millisecond, I allowed David's fear to infect me. But then I remembered Sandy's flinty determination and her words, *I want to live.* I also knew that crises are often darkest before the dawn, and chest infections are a way of clearing out old emotional "stuff." She would make it. Nevertheless, to assist her with her recovery, I sent her a tape of positive affirmations tailored to her specific situation. In my mind's eye, I held her in a bubble of strong, pink, loving light to give her strength as she fought for her life.

For the next four days, tearful phone updates came from Sandy's children. At the same time, confusing e-mails from my stepmother were also appearing. One day my father was showing signs of awareness, the next he had sunk back into a comatose state. Was my father going to live another ten years? At 86, having had two 30-year marriages, he had had a good life. But why shouldn't he live until he was 96 and continue to enjoy his garden and the joy he shared with his second wife, who was 25 years his junior? Both my father and my dear friend were choosing between life and death. A week later, my father finally succumbed to the stroke in his brain stem and other infections. After two months of valiant struggle, he had made his choice to let go and shed his mortal coil.

As I was packing to fly to Wales for my father's funeral, David called. "Mum's bossing us around again." He chuckled. "I think she's going to be okay."

Phew.

In August of that year, as I had promised, I flew out to Nova Scotia to see Sandy and our other friends at her ocean-side retreat, or *Sandyland* as we affectionately call it. In her kitchen, as we feasted on fresh local lobster, I reminded her of our visualization and the deal we had made. "I expect you to do somersaults in the garden," I said.

She laughed. "Well," she said in her most playful voice, "the garden and the vegetables are looking good. Maybe I will." Though she was in great spirits, we could all see the toll the fight for her life had taken on her. While we saw no somersaults, when a hurricane hit Sandyland the third day we were there, Sandy was the first outside in 90-mph winds and slashing rain to rescue her heavy, low-flying wooden furniture. Yes, she was definitely on the road to recovery.

On New Year's Eve 2007, both Sandy and I found ourselves in California. She was working in Lake Tahoe on yet another sales project, so I drove from San Francisco, where I was on a writing retreat, to see her. We had intended to celebrate the end of 2007 with all its challenges, but we were both too tired to tackle the snowy streets and crowded restaurants. Her pine-log accommodation was so warm and cozy, we decided to stay in.

"This has been a hell of a year," I summarized.

"Got that right." Sandy smiled, thinking of her ordeal.

As I sipped on a glass of woody Cabernet in front of the fire, I asked, "Do you remember Angela, my friend who had breast cancer? The doctors have just declared her cancer-free—or at least she's in complete remission. And Joe, my artist friend, not only survived his heart scare but began a wonderful new romance while he was hooked up to tubes in the emergency room." I stared into the fire, thinking of my father, who hadn't made it.

"Amazing!" The reflection of flames flickered on Sandy's wine glass as she took in both these miracles. "Speaking of romance," Sandy said, a small smile curling her lips, "in September, an old friend of mine called me at two in the morning. Apparently, his wife died a couple of months ago and he's been traveling. He wants to get together with me soon. What do you think?"

"Well, he won't be ready for a deep relationship right now," I started, clicking into psychic mode. "He probably needs a confidante more than anything at the moment, but given time it could develop."

We both stared into the fire, reflecting.

"I think it's great!" I added after a while. Sandy had not been involved with anyone for a long time. I sat up. "What's his name?"

"Arthur. He's a retired professor."

"Isn't that what I told you in the last reading, Sandy?" I do *so* like to be right, but more than that, I love my friends and clients to be happy and healthy.

"Oh . . . yeah," she said, finally remembering my prediction, her glass poised mid-air. "But I don't know whether he's *really* interested."

"Oh, come on now. Remember the reading. You're due for a 20-year relationship with a retired professor who travels."

"Well, right now he's travelling a lot to help him get over his wife." She blinked, considering the idea that this man could possibly be the one. "We always did get along great. He's going through grief right now, but we could always laugh and laugh." Now she was grinning from ear to ear.

"Wonderful," I said, excited for her. I thought of my father again. "My step-mother is travelling a lot, too, probably going through the same thing. Just give it time."

"Do you really think . . . ?" She frowned, tentative about the possibility of happiness.

"Yes, Sandy. Yes." I lifted my glass to clink hers. "Whether it's him or somebody else who can make you happy, here's to choosing life and love. Happy New Year!"

18 Why Is My Life Such a Struggle?

Dear Natasha,

I appear to be afflicted with one struggle after another. Why me? Is there anything I can do to change it?

Dear Struggler,

While life is definitely a place for learning, and we all have our challenges to deal with, life is not meant to be a *constant* struggle. I am sorry to hear that you are experiencing all this negativity. Though it is understandable that you feel you have no control over these dramas and you might even feel persecuted, good news awaits you.

You can change the negatives to positives. These unhappy events represent a reenactment of the negative dynamics that have been at work in your life perhaps since a devastating event in your childhood or since your first days on the planet or even since your time in the womb!

Listed below are several possible causes for your subconscious need to reenact these dramas. I also make suggestions for action you can take to shift your energy from a lower to a higher vibration so you can attract success.

❖ You might be magnetizing negative events to yourself because certain beliefs still drive your sense of who you are. The core beliefs that we adopted first as children and that sit in our subconscious minds draw both joy and pain to us throughout our lives. Based on those illusory beliefs, what you *think* you deserve to have or not have in your life unfolds over time. Patterns in our dramas begin to emerge. Like a recurring bad dream, the same old events will be repeated—perhaps in slightly different form—until we finally heal the core belief that seeded the original pain. The truth, painful as the new awareness might be, will set you free to be your authentic self

Action: By identifying the theme of your struggles, the deeper truth, you can release these destructive illusions. Write down what is for you the common denominator in all your struggles. For example, "When I am on the verge of success or happiness, something always shows up to destroy it." Then ask yourself, "What do I believe about myself that would allow this pattern?" Because these are deeply embedded and painful beliefs, you may need a therapist to help you excavate them.

- You may be subconsciously carrying an old guilt from this life or from a former lifetime for which you feel you need to be punished. **Action:** Write a list of possible "sins" you might have committed against others or yourself, deeds you might have done or that you have left undone. Affirm that you are innocent, be compassionate with yourself and others for hurting you. Let the pain of these transgressions go. Burn the paper on which the list is written. As the smoke rises, ask your higher power to transmute this pain into blessings of peace, joy, and abundance for all. If you sense that this guilt arises out of a past-life experience, you will need to seek out a past-life regressionist to excavate those dramas. Always thank your "teachers" for the lessons. This process is very good for your health!
- You may have absorbed the core belief from your environment that life is a struggle or that you don't deserve to be happy.
  Action: Take a piece of paper and draw a line down the middle. In the left-hand column, write down who you were told you are. In the right-hand column, write the truth about who you really are today. Now write up the right-hand column as affirmations. For example, "I am intelligent, brave, and compassionate. I deserve the very best in life." Repeat these affirmations for at least 31 consecutive days. For a deeper impact, record them in your own voice and play them while you drop off to sleep. This process is a version of self-hypnosis and will begin to change your core beliefs and your outcomes.
- Your self-esteem might be on such a low frequency that, because like attracts like, your negative thinking is magnetizing lower vibrational people and events to you.
  Action: Keep a compliment journal. Enter into it all the loving, flattering, and perceptive statements people have said to you over the years, one compliment per page. Write down too what you love about yourself, even if it is "I'm great at creating dramas!" Affirm many times a day, "I deserve the very best because I am the very best. I am getting better every day in every way."
- You might be creating struggle in your relationships and in your life to get attention. Negative attention is often better than no attention at all. This need for attention could also be seen as an unconscious cry for help. Unconsciously you are drawing attention to something you cannot name. You need to identify the underlying pain so the original drama can be extricated and healed.
  Action: Ask yourself what the theme of your dramas is? Betrayal?

Abandonment? Abuse? This is the wound that needs to be healed. From where, when, and with whom did the original pain arise? Since this is your movie, perhaps you need to forgive yourself for abusing, abandoning, or betraying someone else? Acknowledge your own part in your movie. Guilt is mostly at the root of our pain: the guilt of hurting ourselves, the guilt of hurting another, or the guilt of allowing ourselves to be hurt. What is the lesson or pay-off that you need to recognize from this pain? The lessons are always asking us to love ourselves more and motivating us to step into our higher power.

❖ You might be suffering from an unfinished trauma or Post-Traumatic Stress Disorder (PTSD). Each time you are reminded of the trauma, all the terror of it is triggered, setting off a reaction which in your case might unconsciously mean initiating a drama. Your mind is using the drama as a diversionary tactic so that your mind doesn't have to face the original trauma. This reaction is normal, but unconsciously you are sabotaging the success you truly desire. While the drama is a coping mechanism in the short term, you will eventually want to "finish" the trauma so you will not be triggered by reminders. Then finally you can achieve the success you desire.
Action: Seek the professional guidance of a trauma therapist who will help you "finish" the trauma so you can once again live fully in the present.

❖ Your struggles could be karmic. The people who are involved in your "movie" and these dramatic scenes might be teaching you a lesson from another lifetime that perhaps until now you have refused to learn.
Action: Role-play some of your negative events in your mind. Take on the role of the abuser, the abandoner, the betrayer. Instead of playing the usual victim role, you are now in the role of perpetrator. Ask yourself what are you (as perpetrator) teaching yourself by abusing the victim (you)—courage, understanding, compassion, power, and/or self-love? From your perspective as perpetrator, you might see that the perpetrators are actually your greatest teachers and the events are in fact pushing you to step into your own power. On a soul level, underneath all that pain might be a whole lotta love. (Please note the difference between pushing another into their power and empowering another. Pushing is *not* an excuse for bullying or abuse and is often motivated by judgmental perceptions and/or negative projections. Empowering, on the other hand, comes from

unconditionally loving the person as they are and encouraging their growth through a gentle process of support.)

- You might be extremely psychic. If, due to fear, you are not channeling that psychic expression into a creative, healing, or intuitive outlet, the ungrounded energy might be causing havoc in your aura. (This refusal to accept and use my psychic ability was, in part, my story!) Then, since like attracts like, you attract similar chaotic situations into your magnetic field.

  Action: Start channeling that psychic/healing/creative energy. Set your spirit free! Take some creative/healing courses and psychic development workshops. (Check out my website!) Once all that energy is being directed into creation, the negativity and fear will just evaporate.

So, **dear Struggler**, you are definitely not without power in any of these situations. If after using the above techniques the struggles persist, check in with a professional therapist. We tend to heal when we are emotionally ready to heal and we need to be compassionate with ourselves until our spirits find their centers again. How do we know when we have arrived? By all the blessings that start pouring into our lives, a sign that on all levels of consciousness, we are in the flow. We are now ready to receive all the blessings that the Universe has to offer because we truly accept and love ourselves for who we are—a spark of the Divine.

PAST LIFE AND PUPPY LOVE

"Oh, Puppeeee!" Georgia cooed as she knelt down.

Georgia's ever faithful, ever playful, two-year-old, short-haired golden lab lay between us on the beige carpet, his four legs stretched heavenward, eyes closed as if already imagining the bliss of having his belly scratched. "You're such a stinker!" she beamed as she obediently massaged his tummy.

The winter of 1993, frozen snow lay on the ground as it did every February night in the ski resort of Whistler. My roommate Georgia and I had just been bundling up before setting out to join our other roommate, Sandy, for dinner at our usual restaurant when Puppy had demanded his owner's attention. We both loved this dog that Georgia had acquired when he was three weeks old. He had come into our lives despite the landlord's strict "no pets" rule and despite Sandy's adamant protestations. Sure enough Puppy turned out to be an Italian-shoe-chewing, mountain-bike-tire-eating, cardboard-shredding holy terror. But Puppy's big brown eyes and the way he tilted his head oh so innocently to one side soon melted our dog-hardened hearts. Puppy was in.

"Give the poor dog a name," Sandy, the senior roommate, had declared when Puppy was no longer a puppy.

Georgia had pulled a face. "I think I'm just going to call him Puppy."

"You can't call a dog 'puppy' all his life, Georgia," Sandy persisted.

"Yes, I can." The owner stood her ground. "That way he'll stay forever young."

Sandy scoffed. "It's no name for a dog!"

"Get used to it," Georgia, the perennially blunt New Yorker, retorted. "That's his name."

And now Georgia was grinning up at me, mischief in her eyes. I got nervous whenever I saw that look. It usually meant she would soon be getting me into trouble. "Read Puppy!" she dared me.

As usual, she was pushing me precariously close to the edge of some abyss I knew was dangerous but an abyss that, like a lemming, I would inevitably jump into.

"What? You mean . . . *read* Puppy?" I must have sounded a bit dense. "Give him a psychic reading, you mean?" I still couldn't believe what Georgia was asking me to do. Though I had been reading for a long time, my full-time professional psychic practice had only begun two years earlier, and I was still working on my confidence in reading humans.

"Yeah! Go on," she said, giggling now.

"But I've never read an animal before." Then I thought about *Maggie Cullen, the psychic crone I had met when I lived in England. Her claim to fame had been reading pets. It seems that English colonials had often returned to their native Britain with exotic animals acquired during their time in the far reaches of the Empire. This famous clairvoyant would be asked to tune in to all kinds of creatures and their various body parts. But when she spoke about past lifetime connections and karmic relationships with the pets' owners, I had at that time deemed the whole concept a little crazy. However, after she had read my own palms so accurately, I knew that Maggie Cullen was the best psychic and palmist I had ever met. Maybe she wasn't crazy, I decided, just very psychic.

"Okay, Georgia," I said, kneeling down, "but if you dare tell anyone in this town I did this, I will permanently duct-tape your mouth closed." Even as I said it, I knew that my friend was not just the worst secret-keeper in Whistler but also the greatest broadcaster of anything remotely confidential.

"Yeah, yeah." Georgia never took me seriously. Now she sat back on the carpet cross-legged, getting more comfortable in anticipation of the reading.

When I took his paw, Puppy was lying on his side. But then, as if he knew what was transpiring and was preparing to receive information, he obediently rolled onto his back with eyes closed. As I held his soft pads in my hand, I too closed my eyes to "listen" to his energy. Not expecting any images to present themselves, I was more than surprised when a small scene unfolded in my mind, clearly detailed and with the emotions that normally accompany a human reading.

"O-oh!" I exclaimed.

"What? Wha-a-at? Wha-a-a-a-t?" Georgia, the patient one, demanded. "This is so-o-o interesting."

"Tell me."

I hesitated, even though I knew that my silence was driving her crazy. Finally I explained, "I'm seeing Puppy in his past life as a *man*."

"Really!?"

"He's in England, the North, maybe Derbyshire."

"What does he look like?"

"He's heavy-set, not that tall, with thick, silvery hair slicked back with Brylcreem."

"What's Brylcreem?" Georgia interjected, interrupting my flow.

"Disgusting thick cream that men used to comb into their hair to slick it back." To prevent any more interruptions, I carried on. "I see him standing in his kitchen, wearing a white shirt, braces . . . or suspenders, as you would call them. It's a terraced home . . . working class like *Coronation Street*," I added for Georgia's benefit. She loved watching "The Street."

I continued to tune in. "But . . . oh . . . !"

"What?"

"He's . . . ." Tears came to my eyes. "It's so sad." I wanted to cry for the excruciating emotional pain this man was in.

"Why?"

"Just a sec . . . ." I listened and more information came. I saw him standing by himself by the kitchen door, as if waiting for someone to come home. But nobody would. "He's all alone," I told Georgia. "His wife has been dead for a long time, I think . . . but . . . ohmigod . . . ." More tears came to my closed eyes. "He lost his sons in the war—all four of them."

I heard Georgia's horrified gasp. "Which war?"

"The Second World War. They're all dead, gone. And he's in unbearable pain."

Georgia gently rubbed Puppy's belly as the information sank in.

"Oh, I get it," I went on. "He decided to come back as a dog in this life because he just wanted to love and be loved. He couldn't bear to be a human and have responsibilities. It was too much for him. He wants to stay young always and never grow up. He just wants to play and heal."

"That makes sense," she said, sobered by poor Puppy's tragic past. "I knew there was a reason he had to be Puppy all his life."

While I continued to hold his paw and his mistress tenderly stroked his furry belly, the dog lay with his eyes closed, entranced, welcoming the validation of his pain and the healing it brought.

"That's why he loves men so much," Georgia suddenly realized. We had often felt somewhat slighted by Puppy's penchant for leaping up excitedly to welcome strange males instead of running to us.

"And that's why he can't bear to be alone," I added. We had more than one tale of how Puppy had escaped, Houdini-style, from his leash in the garden or from some room in the house, and found his way into the village. Like the animals in *The Incredible Journey,* he could be seen trotting across major intersections, making his way to the hotel where Georgia worked. He would stroll into her office and park himself under her desk as if it were his rightful place. Her employers had long ago given up on keeping him away and now he was accepted as part of the office team.

Georgia and I were also constantly bemoaning what would happen whenever we took Puppy for a walk: we could never go more than a few yards before oncoming pedestrians would stop us to exclaim, "Oooh, what a beeeyootiful puppy!" and kneel down to shower him with affection. While they drooled over him, Georgia and I would stand patiently waiting. Puppy, of course, wagged his tail, panted, and inhaled the unending adoration as if it could never be enough.

And now we knew why.

19 Where Do Our Pets Go When They Die?

Dear Natasha,

My dog died recently and I really miss him. What happens to our pets after they die?

Dear Animal Lover,

Theories abound as to whether animals have spirits and what happens to them when they die. The Hindus believe in a hierarchy of reincarnation: perhaps we begin as ants and work our way up to bats and then on up through the food chain. But no hard and fast rules apply when I am tuning in either to my clients or to the animals themselves. We are all spirit and therefore subject to the same laws of karma. We all go to the same place—heaven—but our perception of that heaven varies greatly depending on our level of consciousness.

Many people who have undergone near-death experiences speak of the presence of animals. Betty Eadie, in her book *Embraced by the Light*, describes how, during her near-death experience, in the tunnel floating toward the light she saw dogs and cats and other animals floating alongside her. Her report confirms my own sense of their afterlife. After physical death, it seems, animals inhabit the same spiritual dimension as we do.

In my experiences as a psychic, I have seen many a deceased pet make spirit appearances in the palms, beside the heels, or in the auras of my clients. "I see a beautiful red setter watching over you," I told one woman. "This animal is also your guide." My client burst into tears, informing me that as a child the red setter had been her dog and her babysitter. Her mother had even entrusted the dog to guard the one-year-old as she played in the garden. Now, 25 years later, the dog was still watching over her.

As humans, we have to remember that we are all animals—just a different species—and not necessarily superior to our furry friends. Whether human animal or other animal, we are all the embodiment of a spirit that has manifested in the physical plane to learn and evolve. Just as our human souls gravitate toward our parents for this lifetime, so are the souls of pets attracted to their owners. A symbiotic relationship of learning between our nearest and dearest, animal or human, always forms.

We might like to think that animals are here purely for their own physical gratification—to eat, poop, walk, romp, and be loved. The task of a pet, however, can sometimes be nobler than we realize. Because they are instinctual and highly psychic by nature and because they love unconditionally, animals often absorb the negative energies of their owners, manifesting illnesses *on behalf of* their owners. Before we assume that our pets—because they don't speak our human language—have less spiritual value than we do, that they are "just animals," we may want to remember that our pets can also be the embodiment of our wise spirit guides, our beloved deceased grandfathers, or even our soul mates. Even after they die, their job is not finished. They not only watch over us from the spirit world, but they will also be there waiting for us when it is our turn to shed our physical bodies and rejoin them in people and doggie heaven!

On the other side of the symbiotic coin, I believe that some spirits—rather than return to life as human beings with all the attendant challenges—choose to be adored pets so they may be free to heal and be healed.

So, dear Animal Lover, animals are in our lives for as long or as short a period as needed. And because they love us, most of the time unconditionally, when they depart, naturally we are devastated by the loss. Give yourself permission to grieve. That kind of loving is not easy to lose. Just know that your pet is not dead but very much alive in spirit. And if you are missing him, know that he is not only missing you, too, but also still loving you from beyond—or from right by your side!

THE CHAIN

"I'm so happy to be here," Shelley said, beaming. She was a pretty thirty-something with clear blue eyes, and a mother of two. The intense determination in her eyes and her comfortable body language reflected the "absolutely-fascinated" category of psychic student and differentiated her from the "this-might-be-interesting" type. She had shown up early for my one-day Psychic Development Workshop with her aunt Laura. Her energy field was wide open, as if she were just waiting to soak up learning like a sponge.

Shelley did not disappoint. Throughout the workshop, she participated enthusiastically. After the first exercise, in which I asked my students to tune in to one another and identify each other's purpose for developing psychically and then share their findings with me, I was easily able to identify Shelley's sacred gifts. It was apparent that she possessed not only a talent for healing small children but also a gift for artistic expression.

"Do you work with children?" I asked her. "I see you surrounded by little ones."

"Yes," she responded, a little taken aback. "I have a daycare."

"Do you do art therapy with them at the moment?"

"No . . . ." Shelley was about to shake her head.

"But she does paint," her aunt piped up, "and she won't admit it, but she's very good."

I love it when friends and relatives validate my intuition, especially when the person I am reading is in some form of denial. *Thanks, Laura.*

"I had a question about that," Shelley said.

"About art?"

"No, the kids. I seem to attract a lot of children with problems. Is that something I am . . . emanating, or is there another reason?"

I focused on Shelley's energy and felt the channeled words flow out of my mouth. "You're attracting the troubled children because you're able to help them." Then I added, "They're lucky to have you."

Shelley smiled, her face cherubic, the child in her still sweetly evident.

"And if you get the urge to study psychology, do it." Her eyes opened wide. "I could see you becoming an art therapist. You have all the ingredients now—psychic ability, compassion for children, and artistic talent. You just need some training in psychology to bring it all together."

"I've just signed up for a psychology course," she breathed, incredulous.

"Great. You see, you do know what your purpose is."

Sometimes, our inclination is to completely negate our inner voice. Unfortunately, cutting off intuition is like trying to pump gas into the car with a kink in the hose. The energy is not going anywhere fast, nowhere it can be used. In my workshops I strive to create a totally safe environment so my students can allay their fears of potential insanity, explore their psychic experiences, feel safe, and "unkink their hoses." Then they can reconnect to the power of their inner voices and give themselves permission to be right about what they feel.

A greater awakening still lay ahead for Shelley. In the early afternoon, our exercise on aura reading unleashed deeper truths. Shelley was the first to volunteer to stand in front of the white screen where we could see her auric field. I encourage my students to seek out more than just colors in the aura. Spirits of loved ones, pets, or other objects of attachment can also be visible in the energy field. Often participants are shy about being the first one to say anything when doing this exercise, so I like to initiate the process by sharing what I see. As I focused on Shelley, I saw the spirit of an older man standing to her right. I watched as he stepped right in front of her and laid a long silver chain around her neck.

"You are being knighted, Shelley," I announced.

She stared at me hard, as if slightly unnerved, and then frowned.

"What do you mean?"

"There's a man standing in front of you . . . putting a long chain around your neck, as if he's bestowing an honor upon you. You've earned it. He wants you to wear the chain."

Shelley suddenly burst into tears.

"Oh, I'm so sorry," I said, walking over to her with a box of Kleenex. The tears of my clients and students are an occupational hazard, particularly when we touch on truths.

"No, it's . . . okay," she said as she took several tissues. "In fact . . . it's . . . it's good." She was shaking her head, trying to regain control.

"Do you know who this man is then?" I asked.

"Yes," she muttered between gulps. "It's . . . my stepfather. He died over a year and a half ago."

Shelley was obviously close to him. But something about her pain told me that part of her grief was unresolved.

"He . . . he gave me his chain before he died. When he was in the hospital, he put it around my neck."

"Wow!" exclaimed one of the other students under her breath.

"But I decided," she continued, "that as soon as my son, who was just a baby then, broke the chain, I would put it away and save it for him for his sixteenth birthday. And when he was two, sure enough, he ripped the chain from my neck and broke the clasp. It's sitting in my jewelry box. I haven't repaired it yet."

"But I think your stepdad wants you to wear it now," I urged.

The tears trickled down Shelley's face again. When she had recovered, she explained, "I can feel that the chain is his way of reaffirming my purpose. He's confirming that I need to use my psychic ability to work with children. That's what I feel anyway."

"Then trust that. That *is* what he's communicating to you." I turned toward the other students, who were visibly moved by Shelley's experience. "Who wants to go next?"

§

Requiring a good rest after a full-day workshop, I was relaxing on my couch the next day when the phone rang. I don't usually answer the business phone on Sundays but something told me I needed to take this call.

"Natasha? It's Shelley. I'm sorry to disturb you."

She was crying again and sounded distraught. I hoped it wasn't bad news. "Are you okay?"

"Oh, yes, I'm fine."

Phew!

"But I have to tell you something."

What could it be?

"My son and I were in the kitchen this morning and he said he could hear Grandpa Jim upstairs."

"Grandpa Jim is your stepdad, right?"

"Yes." She paused and I held my breath. "I told my son it couldn't be him. And he said, 'He is, Mum. I can hear his footsteps.' So then I went upstairs to investigate and, of course, he wasn't in the bedroom. But while I was there, I decided to get the chain out just to look at it." She paused.

And?

"When I held up the chain, I saw that—" The voice at the other end of the line wavered and I could hear sniffling.

What?

"—the chain wasn't broken," Shelley finally announced, exhaling the words. "The clasp was whole again."

What? Wow! The hair on the back of my neck prickled as the implications sank in.

"How do you interpret that?" I asked finally, curious as to Shelley's translation.

"That he wants me to wear it," she responded somewhat shyly.

"Yes." I paused, tuning in to Grandpa Jim for myself, asking what this episode represented. "I think he is also trying to tell you that nothing is broken. Your link with him isn't broken, the chain between this life and the next is still intact, and he is not dead but with you always." I heard a sharp intake of breath at the other end of the line. "But as I say in the workshop, whatever the sign means to *you* is what the message is."

I was gratified by the healing taking place in this young woman who had, at such a young age, lost the only father she had ever known. And though she missed him terribly, she might now understand that the gulf between this world and the next is just an illusion and really not that wide at all.

"So wear the chain and be happy," I urged.

Her soft chuckle wafted down the line. "Thank you, Natasha."

20 How Can I Let Go of Grief?

Dear Natasha,

My sister, who I was very close to, died more than three years ago. Friends tell me I should be over it by now, but for some reason I can't seem to accept her death. What can I do to let go of this grief?

Dear Grieving,

You might be encountering difficulties coping with your sister's death for several reasons. In our Western culture, we don't deal well with grief. Sometimes we don't allow ourselves to grieve and sometimes others can be less than supportive of our grieving process. Consequently, many of us suffer from unresolved grief.

Grief is not only caused by the death of a loved one. Grief can also be caused by the loss of a relationship, pet, job, position, body part, or good health. Yet, in the face of misfortune we are often slapped with the message "suck it up." Unfortunately, if we do hold the grief in our bodies, the dis-ease can eventually make us physically or emotionally ill.

What I would like you to know is that, despite what any of your well-meaning friends or relatives say, the grief process is as personal as the relationship that you and your sister had. Therefore, you need to grieve in the time and the way that is appropriate for you and that relationship.

The following are possible reasons you haven't been able to move forward.

- The pain of your loss needs to be validated. If others—through insensitivity, ignorance, or just plain hard-heartedness—do not acknowledge the depth of your pain, then you can feel misunderstood, abandoned, and alone. Many people don't like to feel pain and therefore have a tendency to try to "fix" you, the griever. The fixer will prescribe a cure for you, will tell you to keep a stiff upper lip, will imply that you should feel better, all so that you don't remind them of their pain. But you still need to be heard. If you are not listened to and acknowledged, an isolation can occur and depression ensue.
  Action: Write a letter about your pain. Dig deep and clarify to yourself what you want others to understand. Once you have the words, select an ally. This person may not necessarily be a close friend or family member but rather someone who will listen and be sensitive to exactly what you are going through. Communicate to them ahead

of time that you need them *not to* "fix" you but just to listen compassionately. You might want to consult a counselor or spiritual healer who is trained in listening.

- Guilt might be keeping you stuck. Unexpressed words of love, forgiveness, or anger between two people can cause a deep sense of remorse.
  Action: I suggest writing another letter, this time to your sister, to express all your feelings about her and your relationship, negative and positive. When it is written, light a candle and say a prayer to your sister letting her know that you want her to receive this message so that you may let go of the unexpressed emotion between you. Burn the letter with the candle, and just for good measure, ask your angels, your spirit guides, or your God to transmute this pain into beautiful blessings of serenity for both of you. Then the two of you can be free to continue your spiritual evolution in peace. (This ritual also works for resolving troubled relationships with the living. Whether you burn the letter or mail it to the intended is up to you.)
- Fear of your own power might be the issue. The denial inherent in refusing to let go of someone or something, especially if they have protected or supported us, often has a pay-off. For example, finally accepting that your sister is no longer here—in this dimension at least—might mean that in some way you have to grow up and take responsibility, perhaps for some fear you have been unwilling to face.
  Action: The question to ask yourself is, "Now that my sister is gone, what is the worst thing I have to deal with?" Then make a plan to deal with that issue. If you need professional counseling, take responsibility and seek out the right person.

So, **dear Grieving**, as in the previous story, understanding that life-after-life is still a process and that spirit is just a thought away softens the physical separation from loved ones, a separation that the living have to endure. The soul's journey and the relationships we encounter along the way are never over. While death has obviously changed the form of your relationship, the bond with your sister is not an ending. Instead it is the beginning of another bond—in a new context. She is now in another dimension, a dimension that is eternally linked to the one in which we now live. What separates us from these dimensions is our refusal to accept that our loved ones still exist in a different form and still love us, often in a more profound and beautiful way. Your sister can still smile down upon you with love . . . and pride. Once we comprehend the eternal nature and magnanimity of our infinite existence, we can find our peace and move forward into our greatness.

A–Z Precepts for a Psychically Open Mind

a. Everything in this universe is made up of energy. Once you understand the universal laws of energy, you can understand the laws of creation—or destruction.

b. You often know what is in your future on a subconscious, unconscious, or even conscious level.

c. If you stop to listen to your own soul, it will tell you all you need to know at any given time.

d. When you are repelled or attracted to another, you are sensing the other's electro-magnetic field (aura). Similar or complementary vibrations mesh more easily.

e. Only seven per cent of communication is verbal. The remaining 93% takes place through body language, thought transference, and sensory perception of the auric field.

f. Physical distance or environment has no bearing on transference of thought. In other words, thought transference can travel anywhere in the Universe instantly.

g. Thoughts are magnets. You can manifest what you focus your mind on, desire, or believe you can receive. "*Whatever the mind can conceive and believe, it can achieve.*" —Albert Einstein

h. The power of your mind can direct your body into illness or wellness, misery or happiness, no matter what the outside circumstances suggest.

i. You can choose your thoughts and therefore choose what to feel. Nobody can *make* you feel anything.

j. You can sense danger without any logical, verbal, or visual physical evidence. You can also sense impending happiness.

k. Your dreams provide you with a picture of your potential future if you learn i) to remember your dreams and ii) to interpret their symbolic language.

l. You can project healing thoughts—otherwise known as prayer—to anyone at any time anywhere instantly. The outcome is determined by the level of intention, the intensity of desire of the sender, and the willingness of the recipient to accept the healing.

m. One person can influence another at a distance with thought if the recipient is willing, consciously or unconsciously, to accept that influence. Apathy is a passive willingness and a state in which you can be manipulated. If you don't have strong mental boundaries, someone or something else can sway you.

n. If you believe in the possibility of a curse—and believe you deserve to be cursed because of some misdeed or feeling of guilt—then you will give it power to manifest.

o. You have experienced other lifetimes that are filed away in your subconscious and in your cellular memory. These experiences can be brought to the conscious level by:

* Past-life regression therapy
* Mental, emotional, or physical "triggers" (e.g., a sore throat triggers a memory of being strangled)
* Memory flashes of past lives (that can make you feel as if you are living in split time or parallel universes).

p. You can, when relaxed into the alpha state, read energy by tuning in to a person's auric field and thoughts. You can also sense vibrations by tuning in to the residue energy left on a person's belongings or photographs and allowing visual images to come to mind.

q. You can choose any tool for divining past, present, and future potentials, for example, Tarot cards, fairy cards, angel cards, I Ching, chicken bones, rose petals, runes, tea leaves, palmistry, astrology, numerology, and phrenology. Or you can just tune in.

r. You were born with intuition and you have the ability and the right to develop it to its highest potential. Its potential is limitless!

s. Some psychics are more naturally perceptive than others just as some artists are more naturally artistic. However, talent alone does not necessarily make them the best. Studying, practice, intention, persistence, and integrity can, however, lead to excellence.

t. You are a spirit on this planet using the vehicle of a physical body for the evolution of your soul. The spirit is not confined to the physical body. It can and does leave the body on a regular basis.

u. You can see the spirits that surround you if you allow your mind to relax and become open to their presence.

v. You are here on earth to love your self, your own spirit, for this lifetime. Just as when you build a home you begin with the foundations so you are here to love the self first.

w. Your purpose as you go through lifetimes is to evolve out of the lower vibrations of fear. Fear comprises violence, aggression, resentment, jealousy, unforgivingness, judgment, guilt, limitation, bitterness, non-acceptance, falsehoods, deception. You then move into the higher vibrations of love which embrace courage, acceptance, truth, gentleness, compassion, forgiveness, integrity, honesty, listening, surrendering, just to name a few. When, eventually, your desire to grow is greater than your fear, you *will* get there. How long you take is up to you. Therein lies your free will.

x. During your lifetimes of evolution, you are destined to experience the light and the dark, love and fear, creation and destruction. Only when you acknowledge the dark can you move into the light.

y. To deny your intuition is like denying that you were (probably) born with a nose. If you do not acknowledge how much you *do* know on the intuitive/psychic level, you will only experience a one-dimensional life. And . . . you'll be left behind . . . to stick in the mud.

z. To develop your intuition, you first need to get to know yourself so you can trust that inner voice and recognize truth when it speaks to you.

Lest We Forget

The physical body
is merely the house
or the temple
for the Spirit
to live in
while it is here
on the physical earth.
The Spirit
is merely a piece
of the Soul
or the parameter
for the personality
through which the spirit can learn the soul's lessons.
The life journey
is to remind us all
of what we already know
so our spirits can return
home
to our souls
having remembered,
having evolved,
forever coming closer
to the Gods and Goddesses,
the Love, Light, and Power
that we truly are.
Remember:
Your body does not speak for your spirit—
your spirit speaks through your body.
Your spirit is not confined within your body—
Your spirit is free to travel universally.
And your spirit is eternally part of your soul.

About the Author . . .

After surviving life in a large, chaotic family in Oxfordshire, England, Natasha Rosewood, a reincarnation of a nomad, found her niche as a flight attendant and apprentice palmist. She traveled extensively and lived in Switzerland, Norway, Germany, and Libya, studying the languages of those countries and picking up a few additional languages before immigrating to British Columbia, Canada. Since 1995, when she finally surrendered to her fate as a full-time psychic, Natasha has evolved from palm reader to psychic coach, facilitating spiritual healing and psychic development through corporate and private workshops, hosting her own TV and radio shows, writing books and columns, and offering private and phone consultations to people around the world. Her mission is to make her work as a psychic coach redundant by empowering others to listen to and trust their own intuition.

Books by Natasha J. Rosewood

AAAGH! I THINK I'M PSYCHIC
(And You Can Be Too)
ISBN 1-4120-2821-3

AAAGH! I THOUGHT YOU WERE DEAD
(And Other Psychic Adventures)
ISBN 978-0-973-4711-1-3

About Natasha J. Rosewood's Next Books

COMING SOON . . .

INTO THE VALLEY OF DEATH (And Other Ghost Stories) is a collection of spooky, fictionalized tales based on the real-life experiences of this psychic and author. Every story, whether set in a haunted youth hostel in France, a ghost town in Death Valley, California, or the alien-invaded English countryside, will have you teetering on the edge of the abyss between reality and illusion.

ABOVE THE CLOUDS is a collection of Natasha's "Dynamic Spirituality" columns, as published in journals and newspapers around the world. This book was inspired by the psychic guidance Natasha has received over the years for her clients and addresses their most frequent issues. The author provides spiritual tools that the reader can apply to these everyday challenges. At the end of each chapter, exercises show how readers can apply these tools in their lives. Whether you want to get unstuck, make a new beginning, or separate peacefully, Natasha's ten-tip programs provide the guidance you just might have been seeking.

How to Order Books

ON-LINE: **www.natashapsychic.com**
(See bookstore locations)
www.amazon.com

BY MAIL: Complete order form (or facsimile) on next page and send to:
Seven Keys Productions
PO Box 1426
Gibsons, BC, Canada V0N 1V0

E-MAIL: **natasha@natashapsychic.com**

SIGNED COPIES: Order from Seven Keys Productions.
Include the name and address of the person you wish the book to be signed for and sent to.

BOOKSTORES: Please contact Canadian & US Distributor:
barbara@dempseycanada.com

E-BOOKS: The following book titles will soon be available in e-book format on my website:

Aaagh! I Think I'm Psychic (And You Can Be Too)
Aaagh! I Thought You Were Dead (And Other Psychic Adventures)
Into The Valley of Death (And Other Ghost Stories)
Above the Clouds

These books can be purchased either as complete books or individual chapters.

NEWSLETTER: Stay inspired by subscribing to Natasha's free newsletter on **www.natashapsychic.com.**

Keep informed about:

Writings
CDs
Books-on-Tape
Radio and TV Shows
Book Tours
Workshops
Speaking Engagements

Book Order Form

Please send:

Aaagh! I Think I'm Psychic (And You Can Be Too)
# of copies __________ Price per copy: CDN $24.99 + s & h

Aaagh! I Thought You Were Dead (And Other Psychic Adventures)
# of copies __________ Price per copy: CDN $19.99 + s & h

Please check **www.natashapsychic.com** for current shipping and handling charges.

Name: ____________________

Address: ____________________

Prov/State: __________ Postal/Zip Code: ____________________

Country: ____________________

Tel: ____________________

E-Mail: ____________________

Website: ____________________

To Be Signed to: ____________________

Methods of Payment:

Paypal	www.natashapsychic.com
Credit Card	Phone/E-Mail
Cheque/Money Order	By Mail

Please make payable to: Natasha J. Rosewood
Seven Keys Productions
Box 1426
Gibsons, BC V0N 1V0
Canada

Blessings and Thank You!